Mark A. Heller

Continuity and Change
in Israeli Security Policy

Adelphi Paper 335

Oxford University Press, Great Clarendon Street, Oxford OX2 6DP
Oxford New York
Athens Auckland Bangkok Bombay Calcutta Cape Town
Dar es Salaam Delhi Florence Hong Kong Istanbul Karachi
Kuala Lumpur Madras Madrid Melbourne Mexico City
Nairobi Paris Singapore Taipei Tokyo Toronto
and associated companies in
Berlin Ibadan

Oxford is a trade mark of Oxford University Press

Published in the United States
by Oxford University Press Inc., New York

© The International Institute for Strategic Studies 2000

First published July 2000 by **Oxford University Press** for
The International Institute for Strategic Studies
Arundel House, 13–15 Arundel Street, Temple Place, London WC2R 3DX
www.iiss.org

Director John Chipman
Editor Mats R. Berdal
Assistant Editor Matthew Foley
Project Manager, Design and Production Mark Taylor

British Library Cataloguing in Publication Data
Data available

Library of Congress Cataloguing in Publication Data

ISBN 0-19-922483-8
ISSN 0567-932x

Contents

Introduction

In 1998, Israel celebrated 50 years of independence with a series of lavish ceremonies and spectacles. But despite the money and effort invested in these festivities, the public mood somehow failed to match the occasion. Instead, there was a curiously understated tone to the anniversary, which was marked more by introspection and unease than by the exuberance and enthusiasm that might have been expected.

At first glance, the understated tone seems curious. Israel had compiled an enviable record of accomplishments that should have been a source of considerable satisfaction and pride. Over five decades, the country had consolidated its precarious independence, won widespread international recognition, absorbed millions of immigrants from around the world, fashioned a powerful army and an advanced military–industrial complex, built a world-class scientific-industrial base, a modern, productive agricultural sector and impressive education and public-health systems. With a per-capita annual income of close to $17,000 by the end of the 1990s, Israelis enjoyed a European standard of living and quality of life. Moreover, Israel had done all this while upholding the rule of law and avoiding the autocracy and civil strife that had afflicted so many other states born after the Second World War. Israeli officials never tired of reminding themselves and everyone else of these accomplishments. Such declarations might have been motivated by an element of self-congratulation, but this cannot be said of the countless foreign observers and analysts, many of whose own assessments were, by and large, not all that different.

But however impressive these achievements, they failed to dispel the discontent that accompanied the anniversary. The organising committee was beset by squabbles, resignations and criticism, and its slogan – 'Together in Pride and Hope' – was received with indifference, even ridicule. An unseemly dispute marred the central cultural event of the festivities, when religious and secular Israelis quarrelled over the costumes of the dance company slated to perform. Israelis reminiscing for the newspapers and television cameras expressed a brooding sense that, for all the progress made, things had not entirely worked out the way they had wanted or expected.

Why this lack of enthusiasm or optimism? Perhaps it is nothing uniquely Israeli, but simply the discontent typical of middle age, national as well as individual. Perhaps it is peculiarly Israeli, a symptom of the congenital introspection of Israelis in general, or (according to many on the right) the congenital negativism of the left, amplified by the leftist media. Whatever the role of these real or alleged predispositions, the reservations felt by so many Israelis were also based on justified uncertainty about the future. For all its gains in national security and international and regional diplomacy, Israel had yet to reach a stable and comprehensive peace with its Arab neighbours. Nor had it achieved the kind of normality in image, self-image and expectations of secure existence that constituted perhaps the most essential aspiration of classical political Zionism – to be a nation 'like all the nations'. Domestically, Israel's achievements were clouded by a variety of concerns: about how the political system could withstand challenges to the principles of democratic government and the rule of law; about whether any social consensus could survive in the face of ethnic/communal divisions, growing social and economic disparities and rising violence; and even about the future definition of Israel's national identity. From these concerns emerged uncertainty about the direction Israel was taking, and doubts about whether the institutions, processes, concepts and myths that had sustained its security policy and nation-building efforts in its formative years were still adequate to the task of coping with changing external and domestic challenges.

This paper examines the foundations of Israeli security policy, and analyses the impact on this policy of changes in external threats and in domestic politics and society. It outlines the major sources and contours of security policy in the half-century after 1948, and specifies those domestic and regional/international factors that account for the basic statist model established during the first two decades of Israel's existence (especially under the tutelage of Israel's first prime minister, David Ben-Gurion). It delineates the conceptual underpinnings and operational demands of the policy of deterrence based on 'offensive defence', and demonstrates how the collectivist nation-building/social-mobilisation model pursued in the early years of Israeli statehood both underlay and sustained the defence effort.

This paper also looks at the changing nature of Israel's threat environment, particularly since 1967. It focuses on the political challenges to the Ben-Gurionist assumptions, especially the assumption of permanent hostility, and on the evolving strategic/operational agenda in the light of the diminishing conventional threat and the emergence of new or more intense challenges: terrorism and counter-insurgency at the lower end of the spectrum, and long-range delivery systems and weapons of mass destruction at the higher end. The overall effect of these changes has been to render the traditional security concept obsolete, and to pose the challenge of reformulating national security policy.

The intensity of this challenge will be very much determined by the political context in which it evolves, especially by the nature of Israel's relations with the Arab world. But it does not depend solely on external factors. It is also related to the way Israel defines itself, that is to its domestic politics and society. Thus, this paper examines the domestic dimension of security issues and analyses the ways in which this dimension both affects, and is affected by, the evolving external threat environment. In particular, it addresses the implications of two transformative changes: the breakdown of the traditional policy consensus caused by the emergence of new ideological streams after 1967; and the breakdown of Israel's traditional social consensus and central sustaining myths caused by ethnic/communal and economic fragmentation. These internal fault-lines reinforce the challenge that the changing external environment poses to the basic security concept, and raise questions about Israel's ability to respond to that challenge. Further changes are needed in Israel's security policy, both in terms of processes, and in terms of structures. These changes include greater reliance on a professional component in the Israel Defence Forces (IDF).

Such changes would challenge the traditional fabric of army–society relations. This issue is intimately connected with the wider question of the overall direction of Israeli society. Israel will have to make a choice, both with respect to its own identity, and its relations with the region and the rest of the world. This paper argues that the basic contest over these questions is between two positions: one inward-looking or 'backlash', the other outward-looking or 'internationalist'. The prevalence of one orientation over the other will have clear implications for Israel's security policy, both in terms of the kind of threats the country will face, and how well it will be able to deal with them. While no decisive outcome to this contest is in prospect, a 'limited internationalism' appears to be on the ascendant. If this trend continues, the chances of Israel achieving secure normality in its second half-century will be greatly improved.

Chapter 1

The Traditional Security Concept

The Conceptual Foundation

Israel was born in war, and ever since has lived in a state of war with most of its neighbours, most of the time.[1] It is therefore not surprising that national security has dominated the national agenda in a way that has few parallels elsewhere. Quantitative indicators – defence spending as a proportion of budget or national product, the extent and duration of compulsory military service, spending per individual serviceman – bear out this judgement of national priorities. So, too, do qualitative indicators; as reflective as any is the fact that the defence minister, unlike his counterparts in almost all other democracies, has traditionally played a more prominent and important role in politics and policy-making than any other individual apart from the prime minister. In 22 of Israel's first 50 years of existence, one person held both portfolios.[2] Security so dominated the Israeli decision-making process that it influenced, and often overwhelmed, almost all other dimensions of foreign policy, and even major elements of domestic economic and social policy.

Given the demands that security has made on the time, attention and resources of Israel over the years, it is perhaps surprising that an authoritative national-security policy has never been clearly articulated. There is no Israeli equivalent of the periodic White Papers or similar posture statements issued by defence ministries or national-security organs in many other countries.[3] This does not mean, however, that something approaching a coherent concept did not evolve. The major contours of a national-security concept emerged out of the political–military leadership's inter- pretation of the strategic environment in which Israel found itself in the late 1940s and early 1950s. These circumstances dictated a posture of military deterrence, which had a defensive strategic purpose, but whose operational content was offensive. This concept has remained more-or-less intact ever since, and from it have flowed the basic structure and doctrine of the IDF, as well as the basic character of civil–military relations.[4]

Israel's security concept rested on a few central assumptions, essentially distillations of the experience of the 1948–49 War of Independence and the interpretation of the immediate post-war geo- political circumstances.

1) 'No Choice'

The first assumption was that Israel would continue to live in a hostile environment. Military inferiority had forced its neighbours to accept cease-fires, and even General Armistice Agreements, in 1949, but these were not converted into relations of permanent peace. The reason, at least according to the prevailing understanding in Israel, was irreconcilable Arab hostility to Israel's very existence. Some attributed this attitude to a hatred equivalent to anti-Semitism. More thoughtful Israelis acknowledged the Arab conviction that Israel was a foreign, artificial implantation, doomed like the Crusader Kingdoms eventually to pass from the scene. They also conceded that the Arab refusal to accept Israel as a normal, legitimate feature of the Middle East stemmed from a political and territorial conflict grounded in a deep sense of injustice. 'Why should the Arabs make peace?', Ben-Gurion is reported to have asked:

> *If I were an Arab leader I would never accept the existence of Israel. This is only natural. We took their land. True, God promised it to us, but what does it matter to them? There was anti-Semitism, the Nazis, Hitler, Auschwitz, but was it their fault? They only see one thing: we came and took their land. They may forget in a generation or two, but for the time being there is no chance.*[5]

But even those who recognised that the rejection of Israel's existence was based on more than unreasoning hatred were no more willing to accommodate the Arab objective of disestablishing the state. As a result, profound Arab hostility was accepted as a given across the spectrum of Israeli politics. This meant that Israel would have to confront the permanent threat of the 'Next Round' – another war with one or more Arab armies.[6] That implied a high and ongoing state of military readiness.

2) Material inferiority

The second assumption was that Israel would have to confront this threat with human and material resources quantitatively inferior to those of its potential adversaries, and with limited territorial depth. This left it vulnerable both to protracted war, because of its limited staying-power, and to surprise attack, because of the lack of space to trade for time. There were three clear implications of this assumption. First, demographic and economic resources had to be increased by reinforcement from outside, as had been the case in 1948–49. Second, Israel had to mobilise its existing resources far more intensively and effectively than did its adversaries. In 1948–49, and often subsequently, this mobilisation effort actually enabled Israel to achieve quantitative parity, or even local superiority, in manpower and firepower. Third, the remaining material gaps had to be overcome by cultivating qualitatively superior military technology, organisation and combat doctrine. In particular, Israel needed to achieve a swift decision on the battlefield. This did not necessarily mean the physical destruction of enemy forces, but it did mean destroying their capacity to sustain combat before outside intervention led to the imposition of a cease-fire. Otherwise, Israel would face the prospect of an early resumption of hostilities, or a static war of attrition along its borders. In short, Israel would rely on the application of offensive force at the tactical and operational levels.

3) No strategic victory through military means

The last major premise was that, however decisive the outcome on the battlefield, Israel would never have either the resources or the international freedom of action to achieve a strategic victory, in the sense of being able to impose its peace terms on a defeated adversary. Since political objectives could not be translated directly into a military idiom, Israel had no political justification for launching a war. Thus, its security policy was essentially defensive in strategic terms. Security policy could serve the political objective of peace only in the sense that entrenched Israeli military superiority could deter Arab adversaries from initiating war and, if deterrence prevailed long enough, compel them eventually to despair of war as an option. As Prime Minister Yitzhak Rabin argued 45 years after the War of Independence, 'the longer Israel is successful in deterring an Arab leader or coalition from being tempted to initiate war, the better become the longer-term prospects for peace'.[7]

Military Structure and Doctrine

These assumptions, and the conclusions drawn from them, had clear implications both for military policy, in the sense of army structure and combat doctrine, and for security policy in the broader sense of national values and priorities. With respect to military policy, they led first to the fundamental decision to build the IDF as a militia-type force or 'citizens' army', rather than as a professional force of long-term or career volunteers. These would form a small, permanent nucleus, with primary responsibility for training and planning. But the bulk of the standing forces would be made up of conscripts (both men and women) recruited for universal compulsory military service. These conscripts, along with the permanent army, would bear the burden of 'current security' – routine, day-to-day deployments and counter-terrorism operations – as well as responsibility for tasks requiring a high state of operational readiness, such as intelligence-gathering and air-power. However, the regular army alone could not provide sufficient forces to prosecute a full-scale war, especially if fighting involved more than one Arab army on more than one front. Thus, soldiers (at least the men) were not relieved of their military obligations following their term of compulsory service. Instead, they were subject to annual reserve duty with some operational duties, but primarily (at least in principle) with the aim of maintaining combat proficiency in the event of a major confrontation. And it was mobilised reservists, especially on the ground but even, to some extent, in the other service arms, who would bear the brunt of any major military effort after the first 48–72 hours.

Given the ability of standing Arab forces to shift quickly from defensive to offensive deployments, Israeli military posture placed a premium on early warning. Moreover, its military doctrine was based on a disposition to pre-empt in the face of any indication that an adversary was intending to use force, or even taking steps that enhanced its capacity to do so. (This is what happened in the 1967 Six Day War, and in its longer-term preventive variant it led to the 1956 Sinai Campaign against Egypt and the 1981 strike against Iraq's Osiraq nuclear reactor.) This disposition to pre-empt stemmed from the fact that a successful Arab first strike might so disrupt or delay the mobilisation of reservists that a counter-offensive would become exceedingly costly, if not impossible, while prolonged mobilisation might cripple the civilian economy.

The need to demobilise reservists also made it imperative to terminate any military confrontation as quickly and decisively as possible. The assumption was that the longer active combat continued, the more political pressure would build on other Arab countries to join the battle. Consequently, Israeli force planning and training stressed offensive capabilities (manoeuvre more than firepower, concentration of force to create local superiority even in conditions of overall inferiority). This was intended to support either pre-emption, or an early counter-offensive to carry the battle into enemy territory. Combat doctrine was geared towards these ends.[8] So, too, was military procurement, even though importing or indigenously developing advanced equipment implied a heavy financial burden.

The Primacy of Security in Foreign and Domestic Policy

Insofar as national security in the more comprehensive sense is concerned, the basic assumptions and conclusions about Israel's strategic environment produced a widespread consensus on the primacy of security. This drove decisions on most dimensions of foreign policy, as well as many aspects of domestic policy. Of course, geopolitical circumstances alone did not explain everything. Israeli policy-makers were influenced by the habits of thought and action instilled by centuries of Jewish communal life in the Diaspora. At one level, the founders and early leaders of the state viewed Israel as a negation of the Diaspora. Hence, their preference for confident, even militant, 'self-reliance' over traditional Jewish communal patterns of passivity, submissiveness and legalism, and the appeasement of more powerful forces or intercession with protectors.[9] But at another level, there was a tendency to maintain the deep-rooted Diaspora feeling of communal solidarity based on the fundamental distinction between Jews and non-Jews, and the abiding distrust of foreigners and outsiders.[10] Thus, Israel's condition was seen as a continuation of the traditional Jewish condition of isolation and vulnerability in a hostile environment, of which the Holocaust was but the most recent, and most horrific, example. Whatever the objective reality of Israel's circumstances, the sense of insecurity was magnified by this subjective habit of thought, which one observer calls 'the gevalt syndrome'.[11]

At the same time, Israel's Jewish vocation dictated a concern for the well-being of Jews, wherever they were. This stemmed not just from the fact that the 'Ingathering of the Exiles' was one of the central sustaining themes of Zionism. Resources were occasionally devoted to actions motivated by Jewish historical or contemporaneous concerns, even if they had no direct relevance to security, and even if they might damage Israel's foreign relations. Perhaps the most dramatic example of this was the decision to kidnap Nazi war criminal Adolph Eichmann from Argentina in 1962 and bring him to trial in Jerusalem. Similarly, the Israeli leadership, especially the earlier generations, retained a measure of commitment to the values which suffused the early-twentieth-century socialism with which most of them were identified. This explained some elements of Israeli foreign policy, such as the decision to cultivate the friendship of newly independent states in Sub-Saharan Africa in the 1950s and early 1960s.[12] These values resonated even more strongly in domestic affairs. Here, the notion of creating a new Jewish society, freed of the social and psychological 'distortions' of the Diaspora, resulted in social-mobilisation policies, such as the encouragement of youth movements and cooperative and collective enterprises, and egalitarian social norms and economic principles, all in the service of 'nation-building'.

On the whole, however, factors such as these were subordinated to security considerations. In one particularly notorious instance, the so-called 'Lavon Affair' of 1954, the security of the Jewish community in Egypt was compromised by the decision to involve local Jews in a sabotage operation aimed at undermining relations between Egyptian President Gamal Abdel Nasser's government and the US. Historian Sasson Sofer argues that the 'almost obsessive emphasis on combining policy with military action often placed Israeli diplomacy at a disadvantage, and such mundane concepts as international trade, human rights and moral issues were pushed aside'.[13]

Of the foreign-policy themes that stemmed from the primacy of security, two in particular stand out. The first was the determination, notwithstanding the ideology of self-reliance, to secure the support of at least one major power in order to ensure a reliable supply of military technology, if not actual combat support, as well as political cover for the various pre-emptive or retaliatory operations deemed necessary to establish and sustain Israeli deterrence. In fact, Israel had no close ties with any major power until the mid-1950s, though it received political support and materiel from the Soviet Union during the War of Independence. In the mid-1950s, it took advantage of French hostility to Egypt, provoked by Nasser's support for the Algerian independence movement, to forge a quasi-alliance with France that produced cooperation in the 1956 Sinai/Suez War, as well as supplies of military and scientific technology. After the deterioration of Franco-Israeli ties in the mid-1960s, Israel benefited immensely from the special political and military relationship it enjoyed with the US.

The second theme was the 'periphery' policy of cultivating security and other ties with non-Arab states bordering the heartland of the Middle East – Turkey, Iran and Ethiopia. The purpose of this policy, beyond general diplomatic benefits or intelligence exchanges, was to distract, intimidate or weaken Arab countries bordering the non-Arabs on the periphery. This aim was also served by providing military support to minorities within Arab countries, such as rebels in southern Sudan or Christians in Lebanon.[14] But the most ambitious example was the close cooperation with Iran under the Shah, which manifested itself most actively in military support for the Iraqi Kurdish opposition. This lasted until 1975, when the Shah decided to improve relations with Iraq and shut down Israeli access to Kurdistan.

With respect to domestic policy, the 'Ingathering of the Exiles' may not have been motivated by security considerations, but the absorption of hundreds of thousands of immigrants, especially in the early years of statehood, had the undoubted benefit of enhancing Israel's pool of military manpower. Similarly, population dispersion, particularly the directed settlement of North African Jews in the north and south of the country in the 1950s, was intended to consolidate sparsely settled areas of the young state at a time when its frontiers were still open to infiltration and borders had not been demarcated politically. Indeed, the link between security and nation-building was such that the IDF played an active role in providing for the transport, housing and education of the early immigrants.

The 'nation in arms' was also seen as an important socialising agent. Universal conscription and reserve service would not only provide a shared experience for Jews from many different back-grounds, traditions and social structures. It would also inculcate common educational values and ideals consistent with the Zionist establishment's vision of the 'new Israeli man'. The IDF came to be seen, not only as an instrument for absorbing immigrants, but also as a way to rehabilitate socially disadvantaged youth, through the creation of special programmes geared to their needs. Finally, heavy state intervention in the economy was driven, not only by a redistributionist philosophy, but also by the need to ensure food and fuel security, strategic industries and dual-purpose international transport capacities.[15] In short, the expansive notion of security blurred the distinction between army and society. As Ben-Gurion explained to the Knesset in 1955:

> *In our case, security plays a more important role than in other countries, and it doesn't depend only on our army … Security means the settlement of empty regions … the dispersal of the population … the creation of industries throughout the country … the development of agriculture … Security means the conquest of maritime and air space and the transformation of Israel into a great maritime power … Security requires economic independence … it requires the development of research and scientific skills.*[16]

The Ben-Gurionist security concept and the military structure and doctrine, as well as domestic policies, that it entailed constituted a heavy burden on the time and resources of the Israeli population. For the most part, this burden was sustained by a strong domestic consensus based on confidence in the political leadership, especially the pervasive influence of Ben-Gurion himself. This persisted long after Ben-Gurion left the political scene. Indeed, his legacy was so strong that it produced what has been called 'the Ben-Gurion complex' – the attempt by other leaders to make decisions based on their guess about what 'the Old Man' would say.[17] But the security consensus also rested on the legitimacy of the military establishment and the esteem in which it was held, and on the social mobility and acceptance that attached to participation in the security effort and in the hegemonic beliefs and norms that lay behind it. Just as important was the widespread conviction that the threat to Israel was genuine, that there was no viable alternative and that the demands and policies implicit in the primacy of security were necessary, and therefore justified.

Finally, the national-security concept endured because it appeared to be vindicated by reality, at least for the first two decades of Israel's existence. Indeed, its greatest success seemed to come with Israel's victory in the Six Day War of 1967. Some analysts have argued that, while the tactical and operational achievements of the IDF were impressive, the very need to fight the war at all stemmed from the failure of the deterrent that presumably lay at the heart of the Israeli security concept.[18] If so, that was a challenge to the traditional security doctrine that was overlooked by most observers at the time. In any event, the victory brought in its train other challenges, some of which were immediately evident, some of which unfolded over a longer period of time, but all of which began to raise serious strategic and national-security dilemmas. These dilemmas remained unresolved as Israel entered its second half-century of independence.

Chapter 2

The Evolution of the Threat after 1967

By the end of the 1990s, Israel was still making major investments in forces geared to fighting a conventional war. However, the threat of a confrontation with Arab armies was no longer the dominant issue on Israel's security agenda. Instead, the country's security planners were increasingly preoccupied with counter-terrorism and counter-insurgency warfare at the lower end of the threat spectrum, and with weapons of mass destruction (WMD) and long-range delivery systems at the higher end. This shift of emphasis stemmed primarily from changes in external threats after 1967, changes which posed major challenges to the traditional security concept.

The Decline of the Conventional Threat

Until 1967, the central operating assumption had been that Israel would continue to face an existential threat posed by Arab armies: the image was of David against Goliath, or 'the few against the many'. The material foundation for this image did not change immediately after 1967. But the dramatic course of the Six Day War did alter the psychological or perceptual foundation. In the first week of June 1967, Israel was a society under siege, its southern maritime border blockaded and its land border threatened by the massed armies of Egypt, Jordan, Syria and Iraq. A week later, the blockade had been broken, the Arab armies were in retreat and disarray, and Israel was in control of the Golan Heights, the Gaza Strip, the Sinai Peninsula and the West Bank, including the Old City of Jerusalem. Although Israel had failed to deter the Arab states from massing forces along the borders and imposing a maritime blockade, thus making it necessary to fight, it had convincingly demonstrated that it could overcome the material disadvantages that had informed its military structure and doctrine since 1949. Indeed, the very scale and speed of the victory in 1967 contributed to a sense of complacency that practically invited the Arab assault in 1973.

The 1973 Yom Kippur War exposed serious deficiencies in the IDF's combat doctrine, including an excessive reliance on heavy armoured formations, with little effective integration of infantry and artillery. In the end, however, even this conflict reinforced the belief that the traditional conventional threat had been, if not removed, then substantially contained. The Egyptian–Syrian assault had begun in the most favourable circumstances for an attacker, with a coordinated operation on two fronts. This caught Israel by surprise, forced it to reinforce the front lines and mobilise reserves while under attack and inflicted serious setbacks and heavy casualties. Nevertheless, the fighting ended with the Egyptians and Syrians saved from an even more disastrous defeat only by a cease-fire imposed on Israel by the superpowers. Once again, deterrence had failed, but once again Israel had demonstrated that it was able to deal with the aftermath of this failure.

Several years later, the material basis of the conventional threat also began to change in Israel's favour, for two primary reasons. One was the end of the oil boom in the mid-1970s. For at least a decade beforehand, Israel had been making steady progress in closing the economic gap between itself and the Arab states. Indeed, the relative improvement in Israel's ability to bear the burden of an arms race with Arab adversaries, especially Egypt, had gradually shifted the overall balance of power in its favour before the 1967 war, and may even have been a factor in Egyptian decisions leading up to that war.[1] Following the oil shock of 1973, the sudden inflow of petrodollars into oil-producing Arab states reversed that trend. But when oil prices fell towards the end of the 1970s, the long-term economic trends working to Israel's advantage reasserted themselves.

The other main reason was the decline in the conventional military capabilities of potential Arab coalitions. This was attributable in the first instance to the Egyptian–Israeli peace process, which began with agreements for the disengagement of forces in

1974 and 1975, entered a dramatic new phase with President Anwar Sadat's visit to Jerusalem in 1977 and the Camp David Agreement of 1978, and culminated in the peace treaty of 1979.

Although the mechanics of this process involved an exchange of Egyptian territory – the Sinai – for peace and mutual recognition, it was stimulated and sustained by conceptual transformations. In the case of Egypt, this involved the abandonment of a national identity and purpose that allowed for no coexistence with Israel under any circumstances. In the case of Israel, it meant the abandonment of a policy that had assigned greater weight to tangible security assets (that is, territory) than to the texture of political relations with Arab neighbours. Although relations did not become particularly warm after the peace treaty was signed, the treaty nonetheless incorporated significant security arrangements, especially limitations on the military uses Egypt could make of the Sinai. The treaty effectively removed Egypt, the strongest Arab state, from the 'circle of war', and turned the only country that had participated in all preceding Arab–Israeli conflicts into Israel's first peace partner. As a result, the southern front, which had been of most concern to Israel since 1949, moved to the bottom of the list of geographical priorities.

The reduced threat from potential Arab coalitions was also a consequence of developments on the eastern front. Until the early 1980s, Iraq had pursued a policy of militant hostility towards Israel, and Iraqi expeditionary forces had taken part in every major Arab–Israeli war except the 1956 Suez/Sinai campaign. Iraq's participation had not made a decisive difference, but the involvement of its forces had slowed the pace of Israeli offensives or counter-offensives in 1948–49 (in the West Bank) and 1973 (on the Golan Heights). The Iran–Iraq War of 1980–88 produced a huge build-up in Iraqi forces, but the struggle with Tehran fully preoccupied Baghdad. While that conflict continued, there was no prospect of Iraqi participation in a war against Israel, and hence no prospect of a viable eastern front. Although the threat seemed to revive after the war ended, it disappeared following the 1991 Gulf conflict and the decimation of Iraq's conventional military power.

These changes did not mean that the traditional concern with conventional threats had completely disappeared. For one thing, the unconsummated peace process with Syria meant that the possibility of renewed fighting on the northern front remained an operating assumption. Following the 1982 Lebanon War, Syria pursued a policy of 'strategic parity' with Israel to compensate for Egypt's 'defection' from Arab ranks, and Iraq's preoccupation with its war with Iran. The objective was to build up enough independent military power to pose a credible counter-weight to Israel without having to rely on an Arab coalition, certainly for defensive purposes and perhaps even to undertake limited offensives.[2] Although considerable progress was made in strengthening Syrian capabilities, this objective was never really achieved, not least because of economic constraints. Even a $2 billion reward from Saudi Arabia and Kuwait for joining the coalition against Iraq in 1991 did not solve the problem of financing the upgrading and modernisation of Syrian military forces. Furthermore, the collapse of the Soviet Union had deprived Syria of Moscow's political, logistic and (in case of extreme need) operational support. Nonetheless, Syria retained a large army of about 12 divisions, and its permanent advantage in standing forces made some Syrian attack scenarios credible enough to require a fairly high state of Israeli readiness. Indeed, Syrian troop redeployments in Lebanon in mid-1996 were misinterpreted as prefiguring a possible Syrian initiative on the Golan Heights, and concern about the costs and political consequences of a clash, if not its ultimate military outcome, produced a brief war scare. Furthermore, as long as the IDF maintained the security zone in south Lebanon, any escalation of fighting between Israel and Syrian-supported guerrillas there could have involved Syrian forces in the country. Even after Israel's withdrawal in May 2000, the possibility of cross-border violence remained, along with the potential for Israeli–Syrian confrontation.

Another continuing concern was uncertainty about the permanence of the changes that had reduced the conventional threat. It was not self-evident that the post-1991 constraints on the rebuilding of Iraqi military power would prove durable. Iraq consistently sought to weaken, harass, deceive and undermine the international inspection regime based on the UN Special Commission (UNSCOM). Iraqi limitations on the work of the inspectors provoked several crises, culminating in the evacuation of UNSCOM personnel in late 1998, and the US–British air campaign, *Operation Desert Fox*, against Iraq. In the wake of *Desert Fox*, the inspection regime essentially collapsed, leaving economic sanctions as the only means of limiting Iraqi power. But the perception that these measures inflicted hardships on Iraqi civilians without undermining the regime in Baghdad prompted calls to relax or end them. If that happened, Iraqi capabilities might well revive before the policies or character of the regime changed. Without a stable and comprehensive peace, the prospects for a broader and more threatening Arab war coalition would improve.

This possibility was related to a still-more disturbing one: that peace agreements already achieved might not last. For Israelis cynical about the sincerity of Arab commitments to peace, 'war after peace' is a problem inherent in the peace process. For others, concern stems primarily from uncertainty about political stability in the region. Many Middle Eastern regimes face threats of varying intensity, primarily due to chronic internal problems: demographic pressures and rapid urbanisation; economic stagnation and stalled reforms; the challenge of radical Islamist or nationalist forces; and uncertain political successions.[3] These problems might lead to changes of regimes which, although connected only indirectly, if at all, to Arab–Israeli issues, could nonetheless have serious repercussions for Israel. That is what happened in Iran, where domestic upheaval transformed a virtual ally into an implacable foe. It could also conceivably happen in Jordan, Egypt or Syria, after a peace treaty based on territorial concessions. (Of course, domestic changes could also produce the opposite effect, replacing currently hostile regimes with ones more neutral or benevolent. But the only place where this seems possible in the foreseeable future is Iran.) If a current or prospective Arab peace partner again became a belligerent specifically because of a change in regime, or even through a reversal of policy by a regime on the defensive, the impact on the conventional threat would be much more significant. This would be particularly the case if the partner were Egypt, which has made noteworthy progress in upgrading and modernising its armed forces since the peace treaty with Israel. But the greatest uncertainty attaches to Syria. Before President Hafez al-Assad died in June 2000, the succession process was unclear and, after his death, there was similar uncertainty about the durability and authority of his son and heir, Bashar. These imponderables explained, not only the Israeli government's insistence on stringent security arrangements in any peace agreement with Syria, but also its determination to press for US assistance in upgrading Israeli military capabilities, including conventional capabilities, as part of any prospective peace package.

Terrorism, Guerrillas and Insurgency

These concerns notwithstanding, during the 1980s and 1990s the conventional threat underlying the traditional security concept yielded pride of place to new challenges. The first was the changing character of the threats at the low end of the spectrum of violence: terrorism, insurgency and guerrilla warfare. Israel's inability to find satisfactory responses to these threats drove it to political decisions that had long been considered anathema: recognising and negotiating with the Palestine Liberation Organisation (PLO) in 1993; and, in 2000, withdrawing from Lebanon without a political agreement with Lebanon and/or Syria, the effective authority there. Nevertheless, the prospect that low-intensity conflict would continue, and would deprive Israel of many of the operational or political benefits these decisions conferred, meant that Israel would be forced to continue looking for effective responses.

Israel had always been exposed to cross-border infiltration, as well as to terrorist attacks on its transport and communications links. Although various Arab regimes tolerated or encouraged such attacks, Palestinians were most directly involved in initiating them and in carrying them out. Until 1993, the Israeli response to the threat of Palestinian terrorism had been two-fold. The first was technical/tactical, based on a combination of passive defences and active measures to harass and disrupt terrorist organisations, and deter or compel the governments of states in which those organisations operated. The second response was political, and aimed at easing Palestinian grievances against Israel, at least with respect to the Israeli occupation of the West Bank and Gaza. But the political content of this approach was consistent only in that it rejected direct engagement with the PLO as representative of the Palestinian national movement in its broadest sense. Instead, Israel after 1967 had oscillated between a preference for the 'Jordanian option' – an attempt to bypass the Palestinian movement by encouraging the maintenance of Jordanian influence in the West Bank and negotiating the partial return of the West Bank to Jordan; and a local 'Palestinian option' – an attempt to confine its approach to the Palestinian question to the population of the West Bank and Gaza, and to limit it to local issues such as 'autonomy' or 'self-rule' under Israeli auspices.

The former approach was favoured by the Labour-dominated governments until 1977. The latter, which implied few, if any, territorial concessions, was preferred by Likud governments after 1977, and found its way into those elements of the peace process with Egypt which referred to the Palestinian question. Paradoxically, both approaches were evident in the international peace conference convened by the US in Madrid in 1991. As part of the negotiations preceding the conference, Israel conceded the presence of Palestinian delegates, but insisted that they had to be residents of the West Bank and Gaza, not formally affiliated with the PLO, and that they participated as part of a joint Jordanian–Palestinian delegation charged with negotiating an interim agreement of the type envisaged in the Camp David accord. The political content of the Israeli approach changed dramatically only in 1993, when the government engaged the PLO directly, first through an unofficial back channel, and then officially, in contacts sponsored by the Norwegian government.

The result of this engagement was the Israeli–Palestinian Declaration of Principles (DOP) on Interim Self-Government Arrangements (the so-called 'Oslo Agreement'). As the title implied, the DOP did not formally commit Israel to a repartition of the Land of Israel and the creation of a separate Palestinian state. But it did rely on UN Security Council Resolutions 242 and 338, which required 'withdrawal from territories occupied in the recent [that is, 1967] conflict', and it did proceed from mutual recognition by Israel and the PLO. It also laid out a practical framework for interim self-government, which specified Israeli withdrawal from Gaza and Jericho, promised Israeli 'redeployments' from more extensive areas of the West Bank in advance of a permanent-status peace agreement, and provided for a functioning Palestinian Authority under PLO control, with a broad panoply of governmental and state institutions and functions. In short, the DOP did virtually everything to incorporate the logic of partition, except to stipulate it formally.

The DOP was made possible only by the election in 1992 of a Labour-dominated government headed by Yitzhak Rabin. But even Rabin decided to deal with the PLO only after he had failed to fulfil his promise to reach an agreement on autonomy with the Jordanian–Palestinian delegation within nine months of his election. In addition, he had first tried to neutralise what Israelis called the 'terrorist infrastructure' in the West Bank and Gaza by deporting 400 leaders of the Islamist *Hamas* movement to southern Lebanon, only to see that move turn into a political and public-relations disaster. Thus, the direct engagement of the PLO was in many ways a measure of last resort, after other alternatives had been tried and found wanting.

It would be an exaggeration to argue that Israel endorsed the logic of the DOP only because of terrorism. Broader calculations were also at work. These included the central importance of an agreement with the Palestinians in helping Israel to deal with the anticipated revival of the Iraqi threat, or the further spread of Iranian-inspired radical Islamism. It is nevertheless the case that one of the Israeli assumptions behind the Oslo Agreement and the decision to recognise and deal directly with the PLO was that the PLO would be able to suppress terrorism more effectively than Israel could. In one of his less guarded moments, Rabin reminded Israelis that in fighting terrorists, the PLO, unlike Israel, would be constrained neither by judicial intervention, nor by the protests of human-rights organisations.[4]

With the start of the Israeli–Palestinian peace process in 1993, there was a widespread expectation that the threat of terrorism would diminish. But the result was precisely the opposite. Beginning in 1994, Israeli cities suffered an upsurge in attacks, particularly by suicide bombers identified with *Hamas*, which undermined public support in Israel for the peace process itself. Bus bombings in February and March 1996 have been widely seen as the main cause of the Labour government's defeat in elections in May 1996.

In Israel, anti-terrorism had traditionally come under the heading of 'current security', that is, a concern of less strategic weight than the overall threat of war with Arab armies. But the political effect of terrorism was so striking that some politicians and analysts redefined it as a strategic threat. In practice, terrorism threatened private individuals rather than the existence of the state, or the viability of society. Nevertheless, the security establishment had no choice but to devote more time, attention and resources to the problem.

The same was true of counter-insurgency and counter-guerrilla warfare. Low-intensity conflict moved to the forefront of Israel's agenda in the 1980s and 1990s in two main sectors: southern Lebanon; and the West Bank and Gaza. The origin of the counter-guerrilla problem lay in the 1982 Israeli invasion of Lebanon. This action was initially presented simply as an extended counter-terrorism operation aimed at protecting Israel's northern frontier against attacks by Palestinian forces, which had installed themselves in Lebanon after their expulsion from Jordan in 1970. Following the outbreak of the Lebanese civil war in 1975 and the collapse of state authority, these forces had undertaken increasingly aggressive operations. It soon became apparent, however, that the objectives of the Israeli campaign went far beyond either deflecting an imminent or developing threat, or establishing or entrenching broader deterrence. Instead, it was, as Prime Minister Menahem Begin asserted, a 'war of choice' aimed at undermining or eliminating Syrian influence in Lebanon; establishing a new, pro-Israeli regime in Beirut; and destroying the PLO's base in Lebanon in the hope of facilitating the emergence of a local Palestinian leadership in the West Bank and Gaza more focused on local concerns, and more amenable to a political settlement based on limited autonomy.

None of these goals was accomplished. The IDF swiftly advanced to Beirut, scored some noteworthy tactical victories over Syrian forces, and even secured the evacuation from Lebanon of most of the Palestinian leadership and paramilitary forces. But Israel was unable to evict Syria from Lebanon or entrench the kind of Lebanese government that would serve its political purposes. Instead, it became bogged down in counter-guerrilla operations, especially against Druze and Shi'ite militias supported by Syria and Iran. In 1985, after three years of inconclusive fighting and mounting casualties, the Israeli National Unity government under Labour leader Shimon Peres decided to withdraw from most of Lebanon, and confine its military presence there to a narrow strip of territory north of the border. After that, the counter-guerrilla challenge was restricted to this 'security zone'.

Even here, the IDF remained exposed to attacks by *Hizbollah*, the most militant Shi'ite party, which took an average toll of 20–25 deaths every year throughout the late 1980s and 1990s. Despite constant tactical experimentation and occasional large-scale escalation, especially in *Operation Accountability* in 1993 and *Operation Grapes of Wrath* three years later, no satisfactory solution to the problem was found. Instead, growing public frustration at the constant stream of casualties made it increasingly difficult for governments to defend Israel's presence in Lebanon, despite the general conviction within the security establishment that unilateral withdrawal was not advisable. In spring 2000, the Israeli cabinet approved withdrawal to the international border by July, whether or not a political agreement with Syria had been reached. By May, the last Israeli forces had withdrawn, and the security zone ceased to exist.

The second counter-insurgency front opened in the West Bank and Gaza with the outbreak of the *intifada* at the end of 1987. Unlike *Hizbollah*'s guerrilla war, the Palestinian uprising was not an organised armed revolt. Indeed, it was not really organised at all, at least at the beginning. It was instead a spontaneous outpouring of frustration and anger at the Israeli occupation, fuelled by political stagnation and deteriorating economic and social conditions. It differed from previous manifestations of Palestinian opposition in two ways: in its scope and intensity; and in its means. Before 1987, there had been periodic outpourings of anger, but ordinarily these had remained localised, and had subsided after a few days. This time, the opposition spread quickly throughout the West Bank and Gaza, and persisted for several years. Second, after a brief, initial period of improvisation, the *intifada*, unlike most previous instances of resistance to Israeli rule, began to take on the character of large-scale civil disobedience, with commercial and tax strikes, the creation of alternative education systems and attempts to organise economic networks independent of Israeli suppliers. This did not, however, mean that the uprising was non-violent. The Israeli occupation had always been punctuated by acts of violent resistance (knifings, shootings and fire-bombings, for example), and these were present, on a larger scale than ever before, in the *intifada*.

The *intifada* never formally ended, although by the early 1990s it had settled down into routine patterns of confrontation. Parts of it, such as the drive for economic separation from Israel, were abandoned as self-defeating. The mass demonstrations, so widespread in the first year or two, became rarer, even as sporadic terrorist attacks continued. But this happened only after the *intifada* had achieved the objective of forcing the Palestinian issue to the forefront of the Israeli and international political agenda. The Palestinian presence at the Madrid Conference bore testimony to the failure of Israeli counter-insurgency policies.

In the West Bank and Gaza, as in southern Lebanon, Israel did not face a national-security threat of the type that had shaped its traditional policy. Here, too, the major concern was the security of individuals, in this case, of Israeli settlers as well as of serving military personnel, rather than that of the state. But again, the inability of the security apparatus to provide adequate responses, along with the controversial nature of the attendant political debate, only added to the sense that the traditional security concept was becoming increasingly out-dated. The need to confront this fact contributed to Rabin's decision in 1993 to inject more coherent political content into Israel's relations with the Palestinians, and to seek a peace agreement with Syria. It also drove the Israeli decision, seven years later, to revive the search for peace with Syria, and to endorse the unilateral withdrawal from Lebanon.

Terrorism and counter-insurgency remained challenges at the turn of the century because Israel could not yet assume either a political settlement with the Palestinians definitive enough to preclude future conflict, or the conclusive end of its problems with and in Lebanon. With respect to the Palestinians, declaratory and symbolic evidence (rhetoric about *jihad*, the pervasive use of maps showing the whole of Mandatory Palestine) and the militarisation of Palestinian society (the proliferation of uniforms and military ceremonies) suggested that future confrontation of some sort was also the expectation, and perhaps the intention, of the Palestinian Authority. So, too, did the organisation, training and equipment of Palestinian paramilitary forces (rocket-propelled grenades, and light anti-armour, and perhaps anti-aircraft, missiles).[5] As a result, Israeli military planning incorporated the likelihood of intermittent but ongoing violence along and across the evolving boundaries between Israel and the Palestinian Authority. While the basic premise was one of low-intensity conflict, this did not preclude the possible resort to heavier weapons and larger formations.[6] Even so, this was not the familiar sort of conventional threat for which traditional offensive pre-emption could provide a satisfactory solution. Not only was it much more difficult to rely on early warning; political considerations (that is, a peace process not yet at the point of despair) militated strongly against such an initiative.

With respect to Lebanon, the Israeli withdrawal eliminated the need for counter-insurgency and counter-guerrilla operations, and Israel's declared intention was to deal with any future terrorist threats through more traditional uses of deterrent or compellant force. But such measures might be inadequate if they are directed against a Lebanese government exercising only partial authority in its own territory. If withdrawal is followed by terrorist attacks across the international border, Israeli security planners will have to supplement deterrence and compellance with other, more innovative measures directed against Syria. However, there is a dilemma, in that diplomatic considerations might restrict the range of measures that could be applied against a Syrian government still formally committed to the peace process. Even if these considerations are overlooked, any escalation of violence with Syria could further complicate the search for a peace agreement with Damascus – the only conclusive solution to the problem of Lebanon-based terrorism.

Missile Proliferation

The third major development in the 1980s and 1990s was the proliferation of ballistic missiles. During the 1991 Gulf War, Iraq launched 42 *Scud* missiles against Israeli targets. Only one person was killed as a direct result of these attacks, although several others died from heart attacks, or as a result of the improper use of gas masks and chemical antidotes. In other words, the ballistic missiles fired by Iraq primarily appeared to affect individual Israelis, rather than national security *per se*. But this is misleading, in the sense that it only refers to physical safety. Because of the passive defence measures taken by the state and at individual initiative, missile attacks seriously disrupted the normal functioning of society and the economy. Schools were closed and large numbers of people fled the major cities for the comparative safety of less exposed rural areas.

Iraqi missile attacks in 1991 also illustrated a kind of danger for which the emphasis on the operational offensive in the traditional military doctrine was inappropriate. For the first time, Israel had been subjected to a military threat to which the most logical response was defensive, not offensive, and in dealing with which the bulk of the military, and virtually all reservists, took no active part. The missile attack appeared to pose a broad challenge to Israeli doctrine by exposing a flaw in Israeli deterrence: the absence, due to political constraints, of a credible threat of retaliation. The circumstances in which deterrence failed in 1991 were so atypical and specific that they may be irrelevant to more enduring threat scenarios. On the other hand, while sporadic missile attacks do not threaten massive casualties (at least as long as the missiles are armed only with conventional warheads), proliferation does allow more distant adversaries to attack Israel without the need to join a coalition including states contiguous to Israel. Remote delivery systems could also delay and disrupt the mobilisation of reserves, make it more difficult to distribute stored equipment, and interfere with air force operations in the critical first stages of a conflict. By threatening the civilian rear area, they might also neutralise Israeli escalation dominance, which played a role in past Israeli strategies of war termination.[7] Thus, missile proliferation poses additional challenges to Israeli deterrence in ways not immediately apparent from the experience of 1991, and to which the traditional military doctrine and posture do not provide an adequate response.

Weapons of Mass Destruction

WMD proliferation was an even more worrying development. Apart from the programmes in Iraq confirmed by UNSCOM, several other regional states have acquired, or are working on acquiring, nuclear, biological or chemical capabilities.[8] WMD proliferation promised to transform the character of the challenges posed by terrorism and missile proliferation, and to confront Israel, once again, with the kind of existential threat to which it had not been exposed since at least before 1967. Israel, because of its small size and highly concentrated population and industry, is especially vulnerable to WMD threats.[9] Conventional terrorism and low-intensity warfare, even if redefined as a strategic threat, may have been viewed as merely painful, protracted and inconclusive forms of conflict, which traditional armed forces were not particularly successful at combating or prosecuting. The spectre of terrorism incorporating WMD is another matter. Concern about this was fuelled by the fear that the further breakdown of central authority in Russia or other successor states of the former Soviet Union would give individuals or organisations access to non-conventional technologies or materials.

WMD proliferation also means a qualitative change in the nature of the missile threat posed by other states, because it places Israel within range of more sources of major damage than ever before. In 1981, Israel had delayed the Iraqi nuclear programme by destroying the Osiraq reactor at Tuwaitha before it became operational. This bought time, but the threat of further preventive strikes of this sort was not a viable long-term response to Baghdad's nuclear ambitions, or to Tehran's. It was even less suited to dealing with their dispersed and concealed chemical and biological capabilities, or those of other states in the Middle East. The role of deterrence in preventing the use of WMD remained a matter of intense debate in Israel, but deterrence as a strategy for preventing the acquisition of these weapons had proved ineffective.

The Revolution in Military Affairs

A final development that impinged on Israel's security agenda in the late 1990s was the anticipated impact of advanced technologies in areas such as communications and precision guidance. Qualitative advances in sensors and in technologies for the acquisition, processing and sharing of data were certain to affect the nature of military command, as well as of combat itself, to the point where many believed that they heralded a veritable revolution in military affairs (RMA). But there was less certainty about how the RMA would affect Israel's capabilities relative to those of its potential adversaries. Some argued that it would work to Israel's advantage, given its more developed technological base, scientific and technical training and experience in systems development and integration. Others suggested that the simplification of vital military functions such as communications, maintenance and long-range/stand-off capabilities would disproportionately benefit those armies with a less developed technical base and more centralised command systems. There was concern that Israel's 'qualitative edge', which had traditionally compensated for its quantitative inferiority, may have begun to erode because of growing Arab (especially Egyptian and Saudi) access to Western military industries.[10] Whatever the case, the technological revolution implied risks as well as opportunities. One of the risks was that societies and military establishments more dependent on advanced micro-electronics were also more vulnerable to 'cyber' attacks.

How these new threats confronting Israel evolve depends primarily on the nature of Israel's relations with the Arab world – that is, on the peace process. Comprehensive peace would make most Arab states less likely to invest heavily in building up their forces, or in acquiring WMD or missile capabilities. In cases such as Iraq, force build-ups are primarily driven by factors other than Israel, but can nonetheless be applied against Israel. In the event of a comprehensive peace, it would be less likely that such capabilities would be brought into play in an Arab–Israeli context, because the political dividend of doing so would be minimal. A political settlement with Syria would reduce the risk of conventional war on Israel's northern front. Since such a settlement would probably also entail a resolution of Israel's problems with Lebanon, the threat of low-intensity warfare on that front could also be mitigated. Finally, a stable permanent-status agreement with the Palestinians would significantly reduce the threat of terrorism from that quarter.

However, while peace would seem to be a quintessential foreign- and security-policy issue, its achievement also depends on how Israel interprets the changes of the 1980s and 1990s, and on how it responds to them. The following chapter analyses these internal challenges to the traditional security concept.

Chapter 3

Internal Challenges

Conflicting interpretations of the national-security environment existed from the very early years of the state, when the consensus was challenged by Foreign Minister and, briefly, Prime Minister Moshe Sharett. Sharett espoused a foreign policy based less on the pre-emptive or retaliatory use of military force, and more on diplomacy and efforts to accommodate Arab political concerns and appreciate Arab cultural sensitivities. In other words, Sharett and others like him argued against the unquestioning acceptance that there was 'No Choice'. But while Sharett had a long and distinguished career in Israeli politics, his point of view remained marginal. In general, the Ben-Gurionist security concept, based on the belief that peace depended on Arab acquiescence in the status quo, prevailed. In practical terms, this meant deterrence based on military strength, without serious efforts at reassurance or conciliation.[1]

This concept began to be challenged only after 1967, not only because of changes in the external environment, but also because of changes in domestic Israeli politics and society – that is, changes in the way in which Israel defined itself. At the ideological level, the Ben-Gurionist concept was challenged by the strengthening of both ethno-national and Sharettist currents of thought, and at the social level by the assertion of sub-national identities and individual rights.

The Fragmentation of the Policy Consensus

The challenge to the consensus on national-security policy after 1967 stemmed from an argument about the centrality of deterrence, and about the role that the territories captured by Israel in 1967 played in maintaining it. This debate involved not only strategic arguments; the emergence of contending schools of thought was also related to domestic social and political processes and ideological changes.

One such change was the introduction of an element of mysticism and millenarianism into Israel's definition of itself. This, too, can be traced directly to the course and outcome of the 1967 war. During the crisis that preceded the outbreak of war at the beginning of June, many Israelis experienced a sense of extreme peril. On the home front, trench-digging in Tel Aviv was accompanied by gallows humour, or by gloomy talk about the destruction of the Third Jewish Commonwealth.[2] Israel's crushing military victory over the armies of Egypt, Syria and Jordan, accomplished within just six days and with relatively few casualties, produced a swift and radical shift to a national mood of exhilaration. The sense of dread was replaced, almost overnight, by one of deliverance. Moreover, Israel now controlled the Sinai Peninsula and the Golan Heights, along with the core of Biblical/historical Israel: Judaea and Samaria (the West Bank), including Hebron (the city of the Patriarchs) and, most significantly, Jerusalem. To many, this sudden reversal of fortunes and the renewed contact with the ancient heartland of the Jewish people could only be explained by divine intervention – part of a process leading, via redemption of the land, to redemption of the people.

This belief was most fully articulated by Rabbi Zvi Yehuda Kook, the head of the Merkaz Harav Yeshiva (religious seminary) and spiritual dean of the Gush Emunim settlers' movement. Kook and his followers argued that the outcome of the war was an essential stage in the divine plan leading to the eventual coming of the Messiah. They provided the ideological spearhead for the settlement movement, which aimed to make Israel's capture of Judaea and Samaria irreversible. Even many of those who did not fully accept this view believed that voluntarily yielding any part of this patrimony would be tantamount to repudiating God's will. In short, the outcome of the war introduced a new element into the Israeli debate on the role of territory in foreign and security policy –

and one which had very little in common with the *realpolitik* that so
dominated the traditional Ben-Gurionist concept.[3] This current was
strengthened during and after the 1973 war, when Israel found itself
increasingly condemned and isolated internationally. Many Israelis
refused to accept that this could be explained by international
norms, or by the national interests of others. Instead, they took
refuge in the belief that Israel had been singled out for a special
campaign designed to rob it of legitimacy. Their response was to
seek reassurance in uniquely Jewish values and historic roots, that is,
in the Land of Israel.[4]

The emergence of this intense commitment to a land-focused,
pre-modern Jewish peoplehood was not strictly antithetical to the
central tenets of Zionism. After all, the ideology of Jewish national
revival in the nineteenth and early twentieth centuries drew on these
spiritual wellsprings, and made potent use of the same symbols.
Consequently, alternatives which were indifferent to where the
Jewish state should actually be located were not only impractical,
but also emotionally sterile.[5] Nevertheless, the institutions built and
policies pursued before and after 1948, under Ben-Gurion's tutelage,
had increasingly emphasised the state-focused nature of the
enterprise. The term used – *mamlachtiut* – connoted a normalisation
of national identity meant to dominate sub- or supra-state identities.
Mamlachtiut was never pressed to its logical conclusion – the full
incorporation of non-Jews into the Israeli polity, or the complete
differentiation of Israel from the rest of world Jewry. But it did stress
the state at the expense of other possible bases of identity. The
outcome of the 1967 war blurred the hitherto clear distinction
between the State of Israel and the Land of Israel. This encouraged
the rise of a kind of ethno-nationalism which viewed territory as an
end in itself, rather than as an instrument to promote another end,
namely security. This constituted a clear ideological challenge to the
state-based rationale of traditional security policy.

The basic consensus on traditional policy was simultaneously
challenged from a different direction, by growing doubts about the
continued validity of the central 'No Choice' assumption. Early
indications of this emerged in the late 1960s, when international
mediation by the UN and others challenged the notion that what
was at issue was the possibility of peace, rather than its terms. The
mere fact that there was a 'peace process', however embryonic,

raised questions about whether indeed there was 'No Choice'. This was the beginning of what one observer termed the 'insinuation' of politics and ideology into security affairs, and the erosion of public confidence in the apolitical basis of national-security decision-making and in the competence of the national-security leadership.[6]

Despite the constant stream of casualties produced by the war of attrition along the Suez Canal in 1969–70, the change was barely perceptible at first, because the positions of the Arab states towards peace were either rejectionist or, at best, ambiguous. The Arab world was still committed to the formula elaborated at the Khartoum Summit Conference of August 1967, which authorised Arab states to seek the return of territories lost in the recent war through a political settlement, provided that it involved no negotiations with Israel, no peace with Israel and no recognition of Israel. Thus, any signs, however subtle, that Arab states were willing to accommodate Israel were hard to detect, and only cultural and literary élites on the fringes of Israeli society challenged the basic postulates of security policy, and advocated a more conciliatory approach of the type identified with Sharett.

Confidence in the wisdom and infallibility of the political–military establishment was not really shaken until the 1973 Yom Kippur War, when 'the concept' – that Arab states would be deterred from any military initiative as long as they could not neutralise Israeli air superiority – was shattered by the coordinated Egyptian–Syrian attack. But even then, the Israeli public attributed the initial setbacks and high casualties to insufficient vigilance, and to the failure of the political leadership to adhere to traditional doctrine by authorising a large-scale call-up of reserves or a pre-emptive air strike. In other words, the fault was still understood to be operational, rather than inherent in the concept itself, or its underlying political premises.

The latter perception took firmer root only following what came to be perceived as the explicit politicisation of military operations. The most dramatic catalyst of this change was the Israeli invasion of Lebanon in 1982. The invasion, dubbed *Operation Peace for Galilee*, was initially described as a limited engagement intended to move terrorist groups beyond artillery and rocket range of Israel's northern border. However, it was partially motivated by, and increasingly seen as, a desire to restructure the Lebanese state and eliminate the foundations there of PLO influence in the West Bank and Gaza. This would presumably enable Israel to implement an autonomy plan with a more compliant local leadership.[7] To the extent that the invasion of Lebanon aspired to produce decisive political gains through military means, it deviated from Israel's traditional concept of the strategic defensive. A successful war would promote a particular political vision inspired by some of the domestic religious-national and ethno-national domestic forces spawned by the outcome of the war of 1967, and swept into power in the elections of 1977. It is therefore not surprising that the war in Lebanon alienated those sections of the Israeli public that did not share this vision. The invasion degenerated into protracted counter-insurgency and counter-guerrilla operations that exacted a continued toll of casualties, prompting growing criticism. It soon became the most contentious war in Israel's history, provoking massive civilian demonstrations, and damaging military morale and discipline; during the course of the war, about 160 soldiers refused to report to their units.

Similar problems emerged after the outbreak of the Palestinian *intifada* in 1987. Despite the different circumstances, the IDF once again found itself confronted with operational demands for which it was not prepared, and the government once again found itself trying to develop and explain a policy that produced a steady stream of Israeli casualties. Since this policy was connected with the shape of Israeli–Palestinian relations – that is, with the peace process – the justification for these casualties, and for the actions the IDF took in its attempts to suppress the uprising, also became matters of intense public controversy. Some in the military, especially in the reserves, were increasingly reluctant to make the commitments that the policy entailed.

For the most part, dissatisfaction with security policy focused on the politicians. In the aftermath of the Yom Kippur War, a Commission of Inquiry exposed defects in the performance of the IDF, but the public generally interpreted its findings as attempts by the government to make scapegoats of leading officers. The same was generally true with respect to the war in Lebanon, although the performance of the military command did come in for some scrutiny.[8] The army's prestige, once sacrosanct, was challenged by the operational demands of counter-guerrilla warfare, which conformed neither with the heroic mould in which the IDF had traditionally been cast, nor with the military's structure and training. Public dissatisfaction with the IDF's shortcomings, though never equal to its discontent with the politicians, persisted throughout the 1990s.

Thus, the obsolescence of the traditional security concept was the result, in the first instance, of changes in the external threat environment, compounded by the rise of ethno-nationalism. The war in Lebanon and the *intifada*, which were in important respects the outcome of ethno-nationalist policies, further challenged the traditional security consensus, including the unquestioned prestige of the army, by imposing a military posture no longer driven by the traditional concept, and calling for military operations for which the IDF was neither trained nor suited. These developments provoked a counter-reaction, in the form of peace protests and demands for policies more reminiscent of Sharett's approach. As a result, in the 1980s the Ben-Gurionist security concept was beset by serious political challenges from two quite different directions.

The Fragmentation of the Social Consensus

The challenges to the traditional security concept were not only ideological; they also stemmed from fundamental changes in Israeli society. One of the major social trends in post-1967 Israel has been a growing scepticism about, and eventual rejection of, one of the central sustaining myths of state-focused policy: the concept of the 'new Israeli man'. Zionist objectives had never been confined to the political goal of creating a state for the Jews. They included a number of social aims, including the 'rectification' of some of the distortions assumed to be inherent in the minority status of Jews in the Diaspora. One of these was an occupational structure that left Jews overly concentrated in commerce, services, intellectual pursuits and some of the professions, and excluded from agriculture, government and military pursuits. In some strands of Zionism, the social agenda was even more prominent than the political one, but even for the mainstream, it remained an important dimension of the ideology.

An even more critical component of the 'rejection of the Diaspora' was the desire to suppress or eliminate ethnic and communal differences among Jews from different diasporas, with different cultural heritages.[9] In practice, this meant not a new synthesis, but rather the adoption and diffusion of the Central/ Eastern European culture of the Zionist establishment.

Before 1967, there were intermittent attempts to give political expression to an alternative approach that rejected the homogenising impulse of the 'melting pot'. This took the form of immigrant parties of, among others, Romanians and Yemenis, but these rarely lasted for more than one or two Knesset terms. Given the combination of a sense of common destiny resulting from the security threat and the various socialisation processes (schools and especially army service), the search for political expression of a particularistic ethnic/communal identity did not ordinarily preoccupy younger immigrants or their Israeli-born relatives. To the extent that such an identity was expressed, this was done largely through immigrant cultural and benevolent societies. Political parties were generally organised along ideological lines and they attempted to accommodate sub-group consciousness through a variety of intra-party mechanisms.[10]

This too began to change after 1967, though not as a direct consequence of the war, and it primarily applied to the political behaviour of Sephardi Jews, especially the large numbers who had arrived from North Africa in the 1950s. Indications of real alienation appeared almost immediately with, for example, the Wadi Salib riots in Haifa in 1953. But it was only in the 1970s that second-generation immigrants began to give focused political expression to their ethnic identity. Although relative social and economic deprivation was a major factor in this development, resentment at the high-handed treatment of their parents, many of whom had been arbitrarily packed off to frontier settlements as part of Ben-Gurion's 'nation-building' project, also played a role. Protest movements such as the Black Panthers emerged, and North African voters increasingly turned to the Likud Party, rejecting the Mapai Party/Labour-dominated Ashkenazi establishment. This was followed by what one observer has termed the 'politicisation of ethnic identity': the formation of identity-based parties.[11] The first of these was Tami, formed by a break-away member of the Labour Party, which gained three seats in the 1981 Knesset elections and then disappeared. The most durable was the Shas Party, which entered the Knesset in 1984 with four seats and emerged from the 1999 elections as the third-largest party, with 17. Although the leadership was religious, Shas appealed to a broader, more loosely traditional constituency as a vehicle of ethnic (especially Moroccan-Jewish) empowerment. In the 1990s, in the wake of the massive immigration from the former Soviet Union, Russian Jews emulated the example of Shas and formed a separate party, Yisrael Ba'Aliya, to promote their interests; in the 1999 elections, there were actually two 'Russian' parties.

In one sense, the Israeli polity had always been fragmented as a consequence of the proportional-representation system that encouraged the proliferation of parties and made it practically impossible for any single one ever to gain a parliamentary majority. By the 1970s, the divisions, which had been largely along ideological lines, began to take on more explicit communitarian and other dimensions.[12] The process of party segmentation was facilitated by a low threshold for election to the Knesset (1.5%) and by a reform in the 1990s that introduced a separate, direct vote for prime minister alongside the parliamentary election. This made it easier for voters to back a party in the Knesset that more accurately reflected their own particular interests or identities, without necessarily jeopard-ising the chances of their preferred prime-ministerial candidate, or leaving the outcome to the vagaries of post-election coalition bar-gaining. As a result, 15 parties were represented in the Knesset elected in 1999, the highest number ever (post-election splits later raised this number to 17). But beyond the mechanics of elections, the breakdown of the party system reflected a declining national consensus over some of the central pre-state and post-independence myths and symbols, including the viability and desirability of the 'melting pot'.

In terms of security policy, the most notable consequence of these social changes was the emergence of a coalition between the forces of Land of Israel-focused ethno-nationalists, stimulated by a sense of relative national deprivation, and sub-group identities (especially among North African voters), encouraged by a sense of relative communitarian deprivation. Support for the Likud among these voters did not necessarily reflect endorsement of its political agenda. Nor did participation by the communitarian parties in Likud-led governing coalitions that included other representatives of ethno-national approaches, such as the National Religious Party or smaller fractions like Tehiya that also emerged in the 1980s. That was explained at least as much by protest against the 'establishment' (the political heirs of Ben-Gurion) and the desire for self-assertion. But it tipped the electoral balance in favour of those forces towards the end of the 1970s, and brought to power governments intent on pursuing security policies inspired by different assumptions and goals than those that drove the Ben-Gurion model.

Another trend was liberalism's growing challenge to the dominant state ideology, socialism. This never translated into the electoral triumph of a Reaganite or Thatcherite government, and all parties continued to advocate principles of mutual responsibility. But even the political heirs of the socialist legacy began to endorse privatisation and other elements of the market economy. This was not just in recognition of the failures of a centralised economy; it also reflected the fact that the Spartan, stoic values and egalitarian ethos of the *Yishuv* (the pre-1948 Jewish community in Palestine) and early post-independence Israel had ceded much ground over the years to individual concerns.

One manifestation of this trend was that, along with a rising general level of material prosperity, economic inequality was also growing. Although the poor were not growing much poorer, the rich were growing much richer. According to the Central Bureau of Statistics, Israel's Gini coefficient (a measure of income distribution in which zero means perfectly equal distribution, and one represents perfectly unequal distribution) rose from 0.319 in 1987 to 0.36 in 1997.[13] In that year, the top 10% of salaried workers earned 11.7 times more than the bottom 10%, and took home 23.5% of all wages in the country; the following year, the multiple had risen to 11.8, and the top 10% accounted for 28% of all wages paid.[14]

Two examples illustrate the nature of the growing social challenge to the traditional security concept. The first is the increasing assertion of individual concerns and rights over those of the state. A major dimension of this trend was the intrusion of various elements of civil society into the national security system. In the late 1990s, Israel witnessed a number of highly embarrassing security mishaps – training accidents, helicopter crashes, casualties from friendly fire, failed commando operations, botched assassination attempts – as well as revelations of financial improprieties and sexual harassment in the IDF. Such events were not unprecedented, but the public awareness of them, and the public response to them, were. The dilution of the security establishment's semi-mythological status after the Lebanon War and the *intifada* meant that it was no longer immune to critical inquiry. This led to demands for greater transparency, and for increased responsiveness to politicians, the media, the courts, interest groups, and even parents concerned with the treatment and welfare of their children in military service. The intrusion of civil society into security affairs was partly facilitated by technological changes, such as direct real-time communication between soldiers and their families made possible by the proliferation of cellular telephones. But it was largely the reflection of broader social trends – a greater awareness of individual rights, and an increased emphasis on them; less deference to authority; and greater openness in society. These changes manifested themselves in, for example, challenges to censorship from the media, more access to more sources of information, greater assertion of individual and civil claims against the state, and more judicial activism. In security matters, these trends resulted in public criticism of the ill-treatment of conscripts and in judicial intervention to block the promotion of officers guilty of abuse or sexual harassment, as well as to enforce gender equality in access to training courses for élite military specialities, including combat specialities.

For the most part, the political–military leadership has reconciled itself to the fact that invoking the term 'security' no longer suffices to dispel scepticism, and ward off criticism. Nevertheless, growing outside involvement in what was traditionally considered none of the public's business has produced signs of barely veiled resentment. There was, for example, a tone of studied reserve in former Defence Minister Yitzhak Mordechai's observation in 1998 that 'there has been a precipitous rise in societal involvement, sometimes even interference, in matters of security. Today, the courts, the legislature, parents, politicians, and above all, the media keep a vigilant eye on affairs hitherto considered to be off-limits to civilian scrutiny'.[15]

The second example of a domestic social challenge to the traditional security consensus has to do with an increasingly rancorous debate about the way in which the defence burden is shared. This in turn reflects increasingly acrimonious relations between the religious and secular populations. Contrary to popular belief, the defence burden was never shared equally. Combat troops served longer than support troops, officers served longer (and did more reserve duty) than other ranks, and those with privileged status were more likely to be assigned to their preferred type and/or location of military service. Moreover, there was always more myth than reality to the IDF's image as a mirror of Israeli society. For one thing, the IDF's role as an instrument of social integration and nation-building never extended to the Arab population. The Druze minority was, with the consent of its leaders, made subject to conscription and served in the army or border police, and significant numbers of Circassians and Bedouins voluntarily enlisted. But the general Arab population was exempt from military service. For another, students in the *yeshivot* (religious seminaries) of the ultra-Orthodox sector of the Jewish population traditionally enjoyed exemptions, or repeated deferrals that were tantamount to exemptions. As long as the security consensus remained intact, these inequalities were not a source of social or political discontent. On the contrary, the sense of threat and 'No Choice', and the belief in the apolitical nature of security policy, conferred tremendous prestige on military service. Influence was actually used to secure more challenging or arduous military postings. A stigma attached to those Israelis who avoided or evaded military service, and their numbers were, in any case, small. Resentment of them grew only when the rationale of the military burden itself began to be questioned.

The problem was particularly acute with respect to the ultra-Orthodox. The original exemption agreement between Ben-Gurion and the political leaders of the ultra-Orthodox community covered only a few hundred students per year. Over the course of five decades, the number of exemptions reached tens of thousands. This was partly due to the higher rates of natural increase among the ultra-Orthodox.[16] But the major explanation was the growing political power of ultra-Orthodox parties. This brought them greater access to state funds, leading to the expansion of the number of both genuine and fictitious *yeshivot* and students, and an increase in the number of exemptions.[17] The result was not necessarily seen as a material loss to the country's defence capacity; the army authorities themselves never insisted that they needed ultra-Orthodox recruits or pressed hard for reform of the exemption policy. But it was resented as a violation of social equity, especially by those who believed that the ultra-Orthodox parties, by allying with the other religious-national and ethno-national forces that flourished after

1967, were partly responsible for the kinds of policies that raised doubts about whether the risks and costs of military service were justified.

These two developments contributed to a third important trend: greater difficulty in sustaining public support for the defence effort, both in monetary and personal terms. Precarious governing coalitions, a consequence of the loss of broad social consensus exacerbated by the peculiarities of the electoral system, made it possible for those with competing claims on budgets to push their demands more effectively. In 1985, the defence budget accounted for over 30% of government expenditure; a decade later, it represented less than 18%.[18] At the same time, the growing focus on individual or sub-national interests at the expense of broader collective concerns reduced the disposition to make sacrifices for security, and led to growing pressure to reduce the share of national resources allocated to defence. Defence spending as a proportion of gross domestic product declined from 10.7% to 7.3% between 1988 and 1998. In the same period, which covered both the *intifada* and the Gulf War, defence consumption fell by over 11%, and dropped from 13.8% of total outlays to 8.7%, while civilian consumption rose by about 60%, and climbed from 70% of total outlays to 73.3%.[19]

This left even fewer resources for procurement and training, and for military research and development, funding for which declined by 43% between 1984 and 1994.[20] The need to compete with the private sector in order to retain officers and non-commissioned officers, especially in technical fields, led to a rise in the proportion of the defence budget going to salaries and pensions, from 19% of the total in 1984 to almost 50% by the end of the 1990s.[21] Coupled with the politically divisive character of some security missions and resentment at how the burden was shared, the growing focus on individual concerns also made Israelis less willing to do longer military service; this figure dropped from 48% of respondents in 1986 to 29% in 1998.[22] Moreover, there was a decline in the willingness of conscripts to enlist for a full three-year stint of service if there were no conscription, from about 75% in the 1970s and 1980s to only 30–40% in the late 1990s. While 60% of conscripts indicated that they would volunteer for a combat unit, albeit not for the full three years, this figure disguised a growing religious–secular rift with respect to motivation.[23] Among graduates of the state-religious schools (where ethno-national values are more strongly held), the desire to serve in combat units was much higher. But in the best secular schools, those known for producing Israel's social, economic and political leaders, willingness to serve in combat units declined by 24% between 1993 and 1998. This is almost certainly because such conscripts, influenced by a broader social ethos of personal self-fulfilment, were increasingly likely to view military service as an opportunity to acquire professional skills and knowledge, or to develop social networks that would be useful in later life, rather than simply as a way to contribute to the security of the country. Combat units, except for the élite reconnaissance units, did not promise that opportunity.

These examples illustrate the kinds of domestic changes that posed serious challenges to the traditional security consensus. The loss of broad social consensus and declining faith in the authority of the national leadership meant not only that domestic support for security policy was harder to sustain, but also that the IDF could itself no longer play much of a role in building Israeli society. Taken together with the changes in the external security environment, these developments exposed the obsolescence of Israel's traditional security concept. What remained was the need for the public and the political leadership to confront the conceptual challenge, analyse and understand the alternatives, and mobilise the will and the resources to adapt policy to new realities.

Chapter 4

Adapting Defence Policy

Security Processes and Structures

Unsurprisingly, the challenge posed by external threats elicited the greatest awareness of the need for change. In the early 1990s, the Knesset Foreign Affairs and Defence Committee established a sub-committee to examine defence doctrine. The Defence Ministry also convened a working group to reconsider the threats and appropriate responses. The IDF Planning Branch constantly reassessed the threat environment as part of its mission to lay out multi-year work plans. As a result, the General Staff has already reordered the list of priorities, designating WMD and long-range delivery systems in the hands of more distant states as the primary threat, with terrorism and guerrilla warfare 'promoted' to second place. The threat of conventional war with the armies of adjacent states, the first priority in the traditional security concept, is now ranked third.[1]

Even before this assessment was completed, every incoming chief-of-staff for at least the past decade had promised to restructure the IDF in accordance with new demands. During that time, several innovations had been introduced that prefigured this changing set of priorities. One was the introduction of a larger defensive component into Israel's overall strategic posture. This has been reflected in procurement and IDF organisation. Israel always invested in civil defence, such as public and residential bomb shelters, but more resources have been dedicated to intelligence and early-warning of missile attacks, and to upgrade passive defences against non-conventional threats. These include sealed shelters, detectors, gas masks and chemical antidotes. The greater emphasis on passive defences included establishing a separate Home Front Command in the early 1990s. Israel has also embarked on an ambitious active missile-defence programme, *Homa* ('The Wall'), of which the joint Israeli–US *Arrow* interceptor-missile project is the most advanced component. There are plans to complement the *Arrow* with a launcher-attack or boost-phase intercept capability based on remotely piloted vehicles, which is also being developed jointly with the US. Work on active missile defences is accompanied by efforts to strengthen deterrence by acquiring long-range F-15I strike aircraft, and developing a secure second-strike capability, perhaps built around submarine-launched cruise missiles. Whatever the precise mix of passive and active defences and deterrence, the response to the missile and WMD threat is almost certain to involve the further development of satellites and other space-based capabilities.[2] The need to integrate all these elements has already provoked debates about further structural changes, and raised the possibility of establishing a Strategic Forces Command or transforming the air force into an Air and Space Command. The assumption that surface-to-surface missile attacks will disrupt the mobilisation of reserves has also led to a decision to strengthen the standing ground and air forces in order to extend the length of time that they can bear the brunt of combat before they are reinforced by reserves.[3]

The missile and WMD threat will impinge on Israel's foreign relations, since responding to it will depend on close technological cooperation with the US. Since the costs are extremely high, continued American financial assistance will also be needed. Iran's flight test of the *Shahab*-3 missile in July 1998, whose range of 1,300 kilometres would put it within striking distance of Israel, prompted the government to revise its spending plans and authorise an increase in the defence budget. The missile and WMD threat may also play a role in the upgraded security ties between Israel and Turkey, which have been vigorously pursued by the defence establishments of both countries. This relationship, which evolved over several years, was given institutional status in an agreement signed in 1996. Although it is not a formal alliance in the sense that either side is committed to come to the active assistance of the other, it does provide for extensive cooperation in a variety of areas:

exchanges of political–military assessments and intelligence; joint naval training exercises; the use of Turkish airspace by the Israeli air force for training purposes; and procurement, technology transfers and equipment upgrades. Turkey shares Israel's concern about Iranian and potential Iraqi missile capabilities, and eastern Turkey would be a suitable location for early-warning and/or ground-based interceptor installations.

Israel has also begun to adapt to the challenges of low-intensity conflict. The experience of both the *intifada* and guerrilla warfare in south Lebanon showed the benefits of having units dedicated to counter-insurgency and low-intensity conflict, such as Border Guard and élite infantry units, as against general-purpose reserve or even conscript forces. The withdrawal from Lebanon eliminated the immediate need for counter-insurgency operations there, while greater political separation between Israel and the Palestinians would reduce the counter-insurgency requirement in the West Bank and Gaza. Nevertheless, sources of possible friction will remain, including the physical intermingling of Israeli and Palestinian populations and political instability in the emerging Palestinian entity, either of which could lead to confrontation. This has prompted a reconsideration of the division of labour for dealing with this contingency. One proposal is to abolish the Southern Command, traditionally charged with both Egypt and the Gaza Strip, and to assign all responsibility for operations involving the Palestinian Authority to Central Command. If this change is implemented, responsibility for securing the border with Egypt in case of crisis or war would be assigned to the Ground Forces Command.

The Ground Forces Command, the successor to the Field Corps Command, was created in the early 1980s as a headquarters framework to develop doctrine and training for integrated ground-force operations among infantry, armour, artillery and engineering units. In 1999, it was transformed into a separate command, with its own budget, procurement authority and logistics and research-and-development capability. It was also given full administrative responsibility for the inventories, maintenance and emergency supply units of all ground forces.[4] The establishment of the Ground Forces Command reflected recognition of the need for better interservice coordination. This was also addressed by moves to integrate the army's independent infantry brigades with its armoured divisions, in order to make training and combat more effective.

However, it was not clear whether these changes portended a plan to invest the Ground Forces Command with operational command authority in the event of actual hostilities. Nor was there any decision to coordinate the 'current security' and wartime operations of all three services in the Operations Directorate of the General Staff.[5] While these mooted changes were a measure of the IDF's attempts to come to grips with the need for organisational, operational and combat concepts suited to the evolving environment in which it would function, they fell short of a comprehensive national-security concept formulated at the highest level of national decision-making. Indeed, it was precisely for this failure to elaborate such a concept that, in mid-1999, Uzi Landau, a former chairman of the Knesset Foreign Affairs and Defence Committee, criticised the defence minister (and, by implication, the prime minister) of the government led by his own party.[6]

This sort of criticism appears to have prompted Israel to begin to institutionalise national-security policy-making at the highest level, by establishing a National Security Council (NSC) directly subordinate to the prime minister. Israel has no shortage of research and policy-planning units. In addition to those in the intelligence agencies, they are found in the Prime Minister's Office, the Ministry of Defence, the Foreign Ministry and the IDF. But critics of national-security policy-making have long bemoaned the improvisational and haphazard character of policy planning. The Commission of Inquiry established to examine the reasons for the failure to anticipate and prepare properly for the Yom Kippur War explicitly recommended creating a body that could overcome bureaucratic rivalries, ensure a comprehensive analytical and planning approach that took account of both external *and* domestic factors, and integrate policy implementation across various ministries.[7] In principle, such a body would make it possible to elaborate and execute a coherent national strategy.

However, the idea of creating an NSC had repeatedly foundered on the opposition of the Defence Ministry, which feared that its primacy in security affairs would be challenged. Only after Defence Minister Yitzhak Mordechai was dismissed in January 1999 did the creation of an NSC became possible. But even then, the fact that the decision was made only two months before a national election and in the midst of a heated campaign led sceptics to suggest that it was more a political ploy by Prime Minister Benjamin Netanyahu than a serious effort to restructure national-security decision-making. It was not clear how profound an innovation the formation of the NSC was expected to be.[8] Nor was it clear how the NSC would operate, if it would do so at all, under the new government elected in May 1999. Its future became even murkier when its first head and founding spirit, retired Major-General David Ivry, was nominated as Israel's ambassador to the US. Several of his deputies subsequently resigned (but then retracted their resignations), claiming that their input into policy had been ignored by new Prime Minister Ehud Barak and his Foreign and Security Policy Coordinator, Danny Yatom.

The formation of the NSC was a belated recognition of the need for a comprehensive approach to the changing national-security agenda. It was indicative of the character of this agenda that the Council was directed to deal with a variety of issues that straddled ministerial responsibilities (such as the architecture of any future regional security systems) and that the WMD and ballistic-missile threats were specified as its top priority. But it was not at all clear that the need for such a body would overcome either bureau-cratic self-interest, or the ingrained preference for improvisation and incremental adaptation over the coherent articulation of doctrine.

The Army and Society

These developments reflected an emerging consensus about the nature of the changing external environment, and produced some structural and doctrinal experimentation. But there was much less agreement about the overall nature of the army that Israel desired. For many, the evolving threat assessment seemed to indicate the need for a more professional military. After all, the advanced technologies and equipment needed to deal with the missile and WMD threat, including space- and sea-based components, will require highly skilled standing forces to develop, maintain and operate them. So, too, will the diffusion of advanced information systems and technologies. Even the trends in conventional warfare will favour highly trained, technically advanced units over large traditional armoured formations, and the apparent requirements of low-intensity conflict or counter-insurgency also point to specialised, long-service forces. All of this suggests a demand for increasingly sophisticated, even esoteric, professional skills, requiring more selective recruitment and the long-term retention of high-quality manpower.

But that would mean much less reliance on general-purpose forces, especially the reservists who have given the IDF its 'citizens' army' character. It would also imply replacing universal conscription with selective service, or even a volunteer force. This might even lead to the privatisation of some technical and/or support functions, by contracting out services such as construction and catering. Indeed, the requirement that some American military-assistance funds be spent in the US means that this is likely to encompass American contractors on a growing scale.

However much such changes might be justified by considerations of technical need or cost-effectiveness, they will encounter a number of obstacles. The first is that the 'new' security agenda has not yet completely displaced the 'old' one. When the multi-year structuring plan known as 'Mirkam-2000' was first elaborated in the mid-1990s, the operating assumption was that the peace process was providing the opportunity to stress long-range force planning and research and development at the expense of day-to-day readiness. But subsequent developments, especially the stalled peace process, revived the concern with short-term readiness, meaning more attention to alert status, training and war stocks.[9] The revised plan, 'Idan 2003', retained some of the initial assumptions, and therefore provided for the early retirement of thousands of career officers, the elimination of several departments and commands and the decommissioning of hundreds of tanks. Nevertheless, the need to be prepared for the outbreak of war meant that these changes would be spread over a longer period than originally anticipated.[10]

The second obstacle relates to cost. Whatever the ultimate long-term savings, transforming the military to meet new threats will in the short term be very expensive. Costs include, not only advanced equipment, but also the benefits paid to those made redundant and the material incentives needed to make an army career attractive to highly qualified technical specialists also in demand in the civilian market.[11] Under Idan-2003, for example, engineers signing on for ten-year projects will get a special bonus of NIS65,000, in addition to competitive salaries.[12]

Finally, changing the IDF into an all- or largely volunteer professional force would make the military an even more specialised sector of Israeli society. The aura and prestige that senior officers enjoy testify to the fact that the career component of the army already has a distinct status in Israel. But transforming the IDF into a 'normal' professional army would endow it with some of the characteristics of a separate caste. This would provoke resistance, if only because of the residual public attachment to an image of the IDF that, however much it may already distort reality, remains symbolically powerful.[13] In all, the requirements and constraints of force planning would therefore seem to indicate, not an entirely volunteer force, but a composite one made up of active-duty career soldiers, and of conscripts recruited more selectively than in the past – on the basis of higher standards, and paid accordingly. Still, even this evolutionary restructuring of the army to meet changing threats raises a broader question of army–society relations that has only just begun to be addressed. This question is linked to the still-larger one of the overall direction of Israeli society itself.

Chapter 5

Alternative Futures

To suggest that, after 50 years of independence, Israel stood at some kind of historic crossroads would be to overdramatise. States are frequently confronted with critical decisions, and decisions deferred often have a way of reasserting themselves. Nevertheless, there was a palpable sense by the late 1990s that old formulas in foreign and security affairs, however well they had once served, were no longer sufficient to deal with the challenges Israel faced. To some extent, this was because the challenges themselves had changed. Even in a strictly military sense, the agenda had broadened beyond the traditional preoccupation with conventional defence to give greater attention to counter-guerrilla, counter-insurgency and counter-terrorism issues, on the one hand, and long-range delivery systems and WMD on the other. In addition, the prospective RMA suggested a major change in the way Israel would have to think about, prepare for and manage war.

Beyond this, regional and international political and strategic conditions were also changing. The end of the Cold War and the Middle East peace process opened up opportunities for ties, including security links, with major states like Russia, China and India. These changes also made regional politics more fluid. One result was the evolution of close ties with Turkey, another the – uneven – development of relations between Israel and the Arab states in the Gulf and North Africa.

But if these developments created opportunities, they also implied risks. One such danger has to do with relations with the US.

In every respect, Washington remains the most important focus of Israel's foreign relations. The complex intermingling of American and Israeli civil societies has few parallels elsewhere, and continuing US political, economic and military support is vital to Israel's pursuit of its interests. Indeed, the changing nature of military requirements indicates that Israeli dependence on American technological assistance will only increase. However, the end of the Cold War removed one of the strategic pillars (however secondary it may have been) in this relationship; Israeli ties with other countries such as China do not always coincide with America's global aims; and the growth of Israel's economy could raise questions in American minds about the necessity for continuing financial assistance. Further progress in the peace process might even lead some to question the rationale for military assistance.

While the failure to achieve a comprehensive peace would obviously imply greater security threats, positive changes in the character of Arab–Israeli relations might generate problems of a different sort, due to the effects on Israel of regional politics. For example, Israel's withdrawal from Lebanon has revived the long-dormant issue of the Syrian presence in the country. If the failure to resolve this issue raises tensions in Lebanon, or between Lebanon and Syria, Israel might feel compelled to intervene in some way. Similarly, a permanent-status agreement with the Palestinians might eventually lead to Palestinian–Jordanian tensions, or might undermine stability in Jordan. As the closest neighbour, such developments would inevitably affect Israel.

Some of these prospective challenges are new, while some have been encountered before. But the Israel that faces them at the beginning of the twenty-first century is far different from the country it was 50 or even 30 years earlier – stronger, richer, more technologically advanced and enjoying a more diverse and supportive network of international relations. This difference obviously confers major advantages in terms of the resources that Israel can bring to bear. But it also includes elements that might prove to be weaknesses. Some of these are the result of material changes, such as the emergence of a high-technology infrastructure that could be more vulnerable to disruption. But the changes with the greatest potential significance have been political and social. The strengthening of sub-national identity has undermined social and political consensus.

And the greater focus on the individual has made Israelis less willing to tolerate the costs of ongoing conflict, or to make sacrifices for the sake of the collective good.

Thus, the apparent need for new formulas to deal with both new and old challenges has been accompanied by an equally strong sense that the choices to be made are intimately connected with questions about the nature of Israeli society itself. These questions too can no longer be answered by reference to the symbols and myths of Israeli state- and nation-building developed more than five decades before, in a more idealistic, and perhaps more naïve, age.

The Question of Israeli Identity

Like many other societies, Israel is in the throes of a 'culture conflict'. This conflict pits two powerful groups against each other, groups that have been described, in another context, as an 'internationalist coalition' and a 'backlash coalition'.[1] The former consists of elements in society receptive to the processes of globalisation, whether economic (openness to international markets, capital, investment and technology transfers); political–military (cooperative inter-national relations, foreign policies of reassurance, restrained military spending and non-provocative defence postures); or cultural (the acceptance of universal, secular values that stress the primacy of individual choice). The 'backlash' group consists of elements that reject globalisation, whether through statist and protectionist economic preferences, foreign and security policies based on military strength and deterrence, or the assertion of unique and 'authentic' cultures and values that stress the primacy of the collective over the individual. The outcome of the conflict between these forces will determine the future of Israel's foreign relations and its approach to security.

This type of 'culture clash' has a long pedigree in Jewish history. Before the destruction of the Second Temple in 70 AD, it pitted the Essenes and other zealots against those more receptive to universal (that is, Greek) cultural influences. In contemporary Israel, it involves two distinct Zionist cultures, one more concerned with the preservation and assertion of uniquely Jewish traditions, the other more attuned to global trends and universal values. This characterisation is an oversimplification, since it understates the importance of sub-cultures: Ashkenazi and Sephardi Jews (and their respective subdivisions), religious and secular (and their respective variants), and veterans and recent immigrants.[2] It also tends to gloss over the degree to which the identities and interests of these groups overlap or diverge to produce constantly shifting alliances. The profusion of sub-cultures has sometimes been compared to tribalism, and its political manifestation, in the form of elections, has been described as 'tribal warfare'.[3] Nonetheless, a two-way division captures a persistent pattern. Analyst Martin Kramer describes the two cultures as secular and religious,[4] though they could equally well be portrayed as modernist and traditionalist, outward-looking and inward-looking, or, as here, 'internationalist' and 'backlash'.

One of the central fault-lines between these two cultures has been in their attitude to the integrity of the Land of Israel; or, put differently, in their views about the disposition of the West Bank and Gaza. Generally, the 'secular' culture tended to approach the issue in largely instrumental terms. This did not automatically lead to maximum flexibility, since security (an instrumental consideration) was often seen to militate against any significant compromise. But it did allow positions to be debated and reassessed in the light of changing circumstances. The 'religious' culture, by contrast, tended to approach the issue in ideological, even millenarian, terms. As a matter of principle, this precluded any compromise. The conflict between these two approaches dominated Israeli politics after 1967. After the 1993 Oslo Accords, it entered into a particularly virulent and violent phase, which culminated in the murder of 29 Palestinians at prayer in the Tomb of the Patriarchs in Hebron in February 1994 and the assassination of Rabin in November 1995. These acts were perpetrated by extremists on the fringe of the 'backlash coalition', though they generated some sympathy among other radical circles. But in May 1996, the entirety of the coalition came together to vote the Labour government responsible for the Oslo agreements out of office.

Nevertheless, the government installed by the 'backlash coalition' endorsed Oslo follow-on agreements (the Hebron Protocol in early 1997 and the Wye River Memorandum in late 1998), seeming finally to have resolved the issue of the Land of Israel, at least in principle. The logic of partition has been accepted as irreversible; almost 75% of Israelis believe that an independent Palestinian state will surely or probably come into being, whatever their own preferences, and over 60% think that the Palestinian Authority's commitment to peace is 'genuine' or 'very genuine'.[5]

But even if the argument between the two cultures about the future of the Land of Israel is essentially over, that about the future character of the State of Israel is not. Israelis will still have to decide which side will prevail, and the outcome will have profound implications, not only for the nature of Israeli society, but also for Israel's foreign and security policies. This is not, of course, a decision that will be made solely on the basis of domestic politics. The fortunes of the different coalitions will be influenced by those of similar coalitions in other parts of the Middle East, especially in the neighbouring Arab states. There too, there are contests between 'internationalist' and 'backlash' coalitions, the course of which will determine the possibility and/or content of peaceful regional relations. It is therefore difficult to assess the extent to which domestic politics drive regional and international politics, and regional and international politics drive domestic politics. Moreover, the contest between the two coalitions is unlikely to result in a decisive victory by one side or the other. Instead, as in many other societies, there is most likely to be a protracted conflict, in which one side may gain the advantage but is unable to vanquish completely, and hence ignore, the other.

This is not, however, equivalent to an inconclusive outcome. It will make a great deal of difference if one side or the other gains and holds a significant advantage. In the first instance, it will determine how Israel defines or redefines itself. In both popular and professional usage, Israel is often described as 'the Jewish state'. This phrase does not accurately express the idea behind political Zionism, nor does it conform to the original intention of the founders, which was to create 'the state of the Jews' – a political construct along the lines of the modern European nation-state, that could give physical protection and political expression to the Jewish people. The difference between the Jewish state and the state of the Jews was never easy to grasp, much less articulate, because of the almost unique overlapping, in the case of the Jews, of the concepts 'people' and 'religion'. As a result, the construction of Israeli political and legal institutions followed a confusing and inconsistent path. The state asserted its Jewish mission or vocation through the use of symbols and historical motifs that could not resonate for non-Jewish minorities: the public celebration of Jewish religious holidays, observance of Jewish dietary laws in public institutions, even the design of the national flag. It also adopted legislation, especially the Law of Return, which discriminated in favour of Jews, and thus against non-Jews. Similarly, the benefits enjoyed by army veterans, such as educational and housing grants or loans and preferential family allowances and other social-insurance payments, are largely unavailable to Arabs, since they are not conscripted. They are also normally discouraged from volunteering, both by the authorities' reluctance to test their loyalty, and by their own ambivalence about their identity as citizens of a country in a state of war with Arab neighbours. But the convoluted procedures that permit the payment of veterans' benefits to ultra-Orthodox and other Jews who do not do military service reinforce the sense of discrimination, which also extends to other areas, such as public housing, land-use regulations and budgetary allocations for local authorities.

On the other hand, apart from pockets of tradition in Jerusalem, B'nei Brak and elsewhere, the secularisation, even 'Americanisation', of society has been the dominant trend.[6] More-over, state institutions and public law have always been decidedly secular. The state's definition of Jewish nationality, for the purposes of naturalisation under the Law of Return, does not correspond with *Halacha* (rabbinic law). The latter demands either a Jewish mother or conversion by a recognised rabbinical authority; the former makes do with descent from at least one Jewish grandparent. So many immigrants from the former Soviet Union with no perceptible element of Jewish identity have taken advantage of the more permissive definition in the Law of Return to gain entry into Israel that the ultra-Orthodox parties (especially Shas) have demanded its amendment to reflect more rigorous *Halachic* standards. But these demands, along with the efforts of rabbis and religious parties to influence judicial appointments or limit the scope of judicial review, have been consistently rebuffed, and state law, as interpreted by the civil judiciary, continues to take precedence over *Halacha*. Even the decision to reserve certain personal matters – marriage, divorce, burial – to the religious courts of the different communities was a concession by the state in order to avoid confronting disruptive questions of principle. But there was always an assumption that the avoidance of the *kulturkampf* that such questions implied, as well as of the equally problematic question of the place of Arabs in a state of the Jews, was a temporary matter, necessary only as long as the ongoing state of war made it too dangerous to confront head on.

Impatience with the status quo has, however, grown. This may be because those who anticipate the end of the state of war believe that this removes the justification for continuing to temporise, while those who believe that the state of war is permanent argue that, after 50 years, it can no longer be used as an excuse to avoid pressing decisions. Alternatively, it may simply be because changes in Israeli politics and society are seen as threatening on both sides of the cultural divide. In any case, both 'internationalist' and 'backlash' elements are pressing to change at least the formal underpinnings of Israeli identity. The 'internationalist' position is expressed by secular, university-educated Jews, including left-wing intellectuals who define themselves as 'post-Zionist', as well as by some Arab politicians and intellectuals. They are urging that Israel shed its vocation as a 'state of the Jews', and become a 'state of all its citizens', fully secularised, denationalised and, like Canada and the US, embodying no particular collective religious or cultural project. On the other side are religious and ultra-Orthodox Jews, who want to create a full-blown Jewish state by imposing Jewish law and practices, rigorously defined, on all public institutions, and at the least on the Jewish sector of the population.

The contest between these competing tendencies is waged on a variety of fronts. One is legal and constitutional. Here, the 'internationalists' press for a complete separation of religion and the state and for a written constitution enshrining the principle of full equality and protection of civil rights and liberties against the state. The preference of the 'backlash coalition' is to impress *Halacha* more fully on the state's laws and institutions. At the very least, they reject a constitution that would formally subordinate divine law to secular law, or separate religion from the state. And they demand that the independence of the judiciary be curbed in order to make it reflect the preferences of the public or the legislature.

The education system is another front. The 'internationalists' urge either the integration of the different school systems (state, state-religious and 'independent', that is, ultra-Orthodox) or greater Ministry of Education control over the curricula of the state-religious and, especially, independent schools. If neither option is feasible, 'internationalists' demand the end of state funding for separate schools teaching parochial curricula. By contrast, the 'backlash coalition' bemoans the ignorance of Jewish matters of the non-observant Jewish majority, and demands more instruction in Jewish religion and tradition throughout the education system.[7] This contest, like others, is not entirely devoid of material considerations – budgets, jobs and other opportunities for political patronage. But it also reflects a genuine difference over the role of public funds in inculcating cultural and educational values.

A third arena is public morality. The 'internationalists', while not necessarily approving of everything associated with contemporary material culture, believe that these matters ought to be left to individuals. The 'backlash' coalition resents the intrusion of Western culture in general, and particularly demands state intervention to eliminate its more salacious aspects in order to protect Jewish values and the public good. The outcome here also has implications for the broader question of limitations on freedom of expression. Whether or not the growing resistance of the media to restraint and censorship will continue depends very much on the course of this struggle.[8]

The Identity Question and Security Policy

The outcome of this contest will be influenced by the course of Arab–Israeli relations. A continuing preoccupation with security, for example, will make Israelis less receptive to the more aggressive assertion of individual rights and liberties against the state, or greater equality for Arab citizens. This will strengthen the position of the 'backlash coalition' in the legal and constitutional arena.[9] But external threat perceptions are not the only factor, and may not even be the most salient.[10] Even if they do influence the domestic outcome, the effect is reciprocal, since the domestic choice will also influence Israel's security and its foreign and security policies.

Were the 'backlash coalition' to prevail, the chances of reaching peace agreements with Syria (and, hence, Lebanon) and the Palestinians would recede, and the treaties with Egypt and Jordan might be jeopardised. Even if agreements were signed, the chances of converting them into stable relations of peace and regional cooperation would be minimal. Israel would remain suspicious of the outside world and would choose – on the dubious assumption that it would have a choice – to remain separate from the rest of the region (except, perhaps, for other 'peripheral' states like Turkey), and from the rest of the world. Convinced that it was, in any case, destined to remain 'a nation that dwells alone', Israel would rely on economic and cultural barriers to preserve its uniqueness. Its security posture would be conditioned by continuing hostility, and would be based on traditional concepts of deterrence.

Israel's ability to maintain a credible and effective deterrent might, however, be undermined in several ways. Changing emphases in education would in the long term damage the manpower pool's scientific and technological base. Before that happened, the evolving character of society might lead to the disillusionment and demoralisation (perhaps even emigration) of those Israelis, such as scientists and engineers, whom the country needs if it is to meet the technological demands of dealing with the problems of missiles and WMD, and information technology. The declining motivation of those not part of the predominant coalition might even make it more difficult to maintain the traditional deterrent against conventional threats. In any case, relatively greater resources would be devoted to defence budgets just when 'backlash' economic policies would be undermining competitiveness and investor confidence.

These developments would be tied to changing foreign relations. The emergence of a more 'backlash' Israel would, paradoxically, damage relations with Jews around the world, and especially in the US, because of resentment in the liberal mainstream of American Jewry at the more exclusionist interpretation of legitimate Jewishness that would prevail in Israel.[11] This would widen the gap between the US and an Israel seen less and less as an integral part of the community of market-oriented liberal democracies. In those circumstances, it would become harder to compartmentalise the security component of the US–Israeli relationship, just when economic and technological support from the US would be becoming more important then ever.

By contrast, the strengthening of 'internationalist' forces and policies would enhance the chances of achieving peace agreements, to the extent that they depend on Israeli choices, because Israel would pursue a more instrumentalist approach to the issue of territory. An 'internationalist coalition' would also make it more likely that treaties could be converted into durable relations of peace, because of its more receptive attitude to economic and cultural openness. Israel's relations with the region would take the form of normal ties with the neighbouring Arab states, perhaps facilitated by the fuller integration of Israeli Arabs into the Israeli polity. In defence policy, Israel might participate in regional alignments or alliances. More ambitiously, it might even play a part in evolving regional security structures, implying greater reliance on cooperative security policies built more around conventional and non-conventional arms control and confidence- and security-building measures, and less on traditional deterrence. Finally, a more 'internationalist' Israel would continue to enjoy a 'special relationship' with the US, while many of the obstacles to harmonious relations with other countries would be removed. One particularly significant consequence of this might be the injection of more substance into Israel's 'privileged status' with the European Union, or even its conversion into some kind of associate membership.

These scenarios overstate the contrast between the two competing camps, and the future is likely to be more ambiguous. For example, a stronger 'internationalist' current in Israel could also undermine Israeli ties with the world Jewish community by diluting Israel's Jewish identity. Similarly, a more 'internationalist' Israel might be more willing to experiment with cooperative security and policies of reassurance, but there is little likelihood that it would forgo deterrence altogether. Even in territorially 'generous' peace agreements (to which they are certainly more well-disposed), 'internationalists' have insisted on asymmetric security arrangements, and will continue to do so. It is unlikely that any but the most committed of 'internationalist' idealists would casually dismiss the vindication of the Ben-Gurionist concept – that deterrence was needed to make peace possible – or the affirmation of its post-peace corollary – that continuing deterrence will be needed to make it durable.

This does not mean that there would be no differences in the nature of the deterrent posture. 'Internationalists' might be more sensitive to the problems of some rhetorical or operational methods, especially pre-emption or disproportionate retaliation, traditionally used to establish and entrench Israeli deterrence. But 'backlash' coalitions, presumably more sceptical about the value of peace agreements, have already demonstrated that they, too, appreciate the need to pursue more circumspectly the deterrence of countries formally at peace, or even committed to a formal but sterile peace process. This explains why, after the 1991 Madrid Conference, Israel, even under Likud governments, refrained from attacking Syrian forces in an effort to compel Damascus to restrain *Hizbollah* and end the proxy war in Lebanon. As one analyst puts it: 'Every time they [the Arab states] extend a morsel of political legitimacy to the Jewish state, they delegitimise to the same degree its strategic practice'.[12]

Even the most determined of Israeli 'internationalists' would find that Israeli 'integration' into the Middle East could not proceed quickly or smoothly. Even in what should be a 'neutral' and beneficial area like economic cooperation, the impact of an 'internationalist' or 'backlash' trend in Israel should not be exaggerated. For one thing, the Arab market is too small to offer Israeli exporters more attractive opportunities than those that already exist, or that will open up elsewhere in the world. Over the course of several decades of Arab boycott, the Israeli economy developed in order to exploit comparative advantages in niches in the large North American, European and East Asian markets. Most of these niches depend on Israeli access to production inputs and on exports of high-value-added goods. There is little supply of these inputs from Arab states, and little demand in the Arab market for these goods and services. As a result, there are few obvious areas of mutual benefit, with agricultural technology and energy being among the most significant exceptions. Of those areas that do exist, some provoke resistance in Israel. For example, there is reluctance to 'export' jobs by investing in Arab countries, or to import large numbers of Arab 'guest workers' to replace the tens of thousands of Eastern Europeans, Asians and Africans who now make up much of the skilled or semi-skilled workforce.[13] Some areas are resisted in Arab countries, because of apprehension about possible Israeli 'economic hegemony' resulting from ownership or management of projects in Arab states. This is one explanation for the sceptical response, both from Israelis and from Arabs, to perhaps the most 'internationalist' vision ever put forward by an Israeli leader: Shimon Peres' idea of 'The New Middle East', which centred on close economic interaction among regional governments and civil societies. Moreover, economic liberalisation, though promoted with various degrees of enthusiasm and determination in the Arab world, has been hampered by, for example, bureaucrats and 'crony capitalists' with a vested interest in state monopolies and regulatory or protectionist policies. As a result, structural reform by Israel's Arab neighbours has been only intermittently pursued, and there has been little movement even towards patterns of economic integration that would exclude Israel, such as an inter-Arab common market. The idea of a Mediterranean free-trade area, originally endorsed as part of the Euro-Mediterranean Partnership established at Barcelona in 1995, has been beset by foot-dragging.

Israeli and Arab political systems also show few signs of converging. Some Arab states, Syria and Iraq in particular, have barely begun to contemplate the notion of political or economic openness. Others have tentatively experimented with greater political accountability and participation, only to draw back when confronted with palpable challenges to government authority. Local resistance to cultural intrusion by the West has left regimes on the defensive and prompted them, in the name of morality or authenticity as well as self-preservation, to maintain or strengthen controls. This is true even in Egypt. In the 1970s, at a time when few could imagine the end of the Cold War, Sadat ended his country's long-standing dependence on the Soviet Union and tried to improve relations with the West, and also began to dismantle many of the controls of Nasserist rule. In economics, the regime experimented with *infitah* (the opening up of the economy to private enterprise and foreign investment). In Arab–Israeli relations, Cairo broke with the Arab consensus and made peace with Israel. But challenges to the regime by both Islamist forces and civil or human-rights movements have led to greater restrictions on the media and non-governmental organisations (NGOs), and to renewed restraints on open political competition. The same is true in Jordan and Kuwait, and in the West Bank and Gaza, where NGOs, which had thrived in the 1980s and early 1990s, were restricted and financially constrained following the establishment of the Palestinian Authority in 1994.[14]

There is still considerable resistance in the Arab world, even where peace agreements have been signed or at least endorsed as a 'strategic choice', to the idea of transforming agreements reached out of calculated interest into fully fledged and enduring peaceful coexistence. This is evident from the negative or apprehensive response among Arab élites (apart from the private business sector) to Peres' 'New Middle East' idea. For their part, Israeli inter-nationalists continue to see the West as their primary cultural referent, and this may temper their enthusiasm for integration with the rest of the Middle East if it means anything other than the pursuit of normal relations, without the need to embrace the region's predominant language and religion, as well as its social and political norms. True, parallel orientations – Western, modern, universal, European, Mediterranean, or any other term for cultural neutrality – would presumably at least provide some common ground with Arab 'internationalists'. Yet it is precisely those elements, at least insofar as associations of professionals and intellectuals represent them, that have most vigorously opposed the normalisation of contacts between civil societies.

All of this points to a broad constraint on the ability of an 'internationalist' Israel to integrate into the region: the persistence of strong 'backlash' elements in the governing coalitions and societies of the surrounding Arab states. Thus, even a more 'internationalist' Israel would probably find itself strengthening ties most with regional states like Turkey, whose political and economic systems, for all the differences, most resemble its own. A comprehensive peace, presumably facilitated by a more 'internationalist' Israel, might improve the prospects for 'internationalist coalitions' elsewhere in the region. But a real Israeli breakthrough with Arab neighbours, even in conditions of peaceful coexistence, would have to await greater successes by counterpart coalitions in those countries, as well.

Conclusion

Towards 'Limited Internationalism'?

The 'internationalist'–'backlash' contest is likely to have no clear-cut outcome one way or the other. Many Israelis sympathise to some degree with some of the ideas represented by both camps, but fully identify with neither. The bulk of Israeli Jews do not define themselves as 'post-Zionists', or reject the continuing legitimacy of the Zionist enterprise, including the need for Israel to express some special Jewish character or mission. Even if personally non-observant, many Israelis generally identify with the Jewish historical tradition and respect and appreciate religion's special place within it. At the same time, they reject the notion of an intrinsic contradiction between a liberal or democratic state, and a state that retains its Jewish vocation and character. And they accept, even if they do not aggressively insist, that civil liberties and social rights can and should be promoted in a more egalitarian way. What they therefore seek is not a theoretical resolution of a conundrum, but a practical formula that can better accommodate these needs – even if that formula entails compromises and inconsistencies. Because of this ambivalence, the most likely outcome of the contest is no outcome at all, at least in the sense of a clear-cut and decisive triumph of either the 'internationalists' or the 'backlash coalition'. Rather, the prospects are for a relative strengthening of one tendency at the expense of the other, manifested in governments and policies that brim with contradictions, but that nevertheless reflect an identifiable trend.

One such identifiable trend emerged in the 1996 election that brought to power a governing coalition more strongly infused with 'backlash' values. The 1999 election, by contrast, appeared to produce a rather different result. The 1996 poll was essentially a referendum on the Israeli–Palestinian peace process, and it resulted in a victory for the chief critic of the Oslo Agreement, Likud opposition leader Benjamin Netanyahu. Netanyahu's margin of victory over Peres was narrow – less than 1% of the total vote – but the shadow of a recent wave of terrorist attacks did give him a clear majority among Jewish voters. Netanyahu was able to assemble a parliamentary coalition of 66 Knesset members, 55 of whom were from parties identified with ethno-nationalist and/or religious values – Likud, Shas, the National Religious Party, and United Torah Judaism.[1]

The 1999 election was held in quite different circumstances. The emotional atmosphere was less charged, not only because of the relative absence of terrorist incidents, but also because the Labour Party candidate, Ehud Barak, portrayed himself as a centrist advocate of peace with security concerns uppermost in his mind. As a result, the peace process was not nearly as divisive an issue as it had been in 1996, and Netanyahu – who had himself approved two agreements involving territorial concessions to the Palestinians during his term of office – was unable to demonstrate a stark contrast between his own approach and that of Barak. Instead, the election became a referendum on the overall political, social, economic and ethical performance of Netanyahu's government (including its attitude towards the rule of law) and on his own character, competence and governing methods. The result of this referendum was a large margin of victory for Barak – more than 12% – including a majority among Jewish voters. Moreover, the distribution of Knesset seats reflected a decline in support for the 'backlash' parties, from 55 in 1996 to 54 in 1999. The strength of the 'internationalist' camp (Labour [One Israel], Meretz, and two new parties, Shinui–The Secular Movement and the Centre Party) increased from 43 seats to 48.

The extent of change was, however, less than was suggested by the magnitude of Barak's personal victory, or even by the shift in the distribution of Knesset seats. For one thing, Barak was not an avowed internationalist, an aggressive secularist or a 'post-Zionist', and he made a determined effort to ensure that he could not be portrayed as such, lest he alienate critical voters in the middle of the ideological spectrum. For another, the Knesset results were ambiguous. For example, the Knesset representation of the 'Russian vote', which had constituted the 'left wing' of the previous coalition, increased from seven to ten seats, but this time two 'Russian' parties were elected. One, 'Israel Is Our Home', made a strong appeal to ethno-nationalist sentiment and gained four seats. The other, Natan Sharansky's Yisrael Be'Aliyah Party, joined the Barak-led coalition with the apparent intention of guarding the right flank this time, but two of its six members abandoned Sharansky shortly after the election because they advocated a more conciliatory policy than he was prepared to endorse. In general, immigrants from the former Soviet Union, who numbered close to a million by the end of the 1990s, constitute something of an anomaly, since they straddle the 'internationalist'–'backlash' divide. On the one hand, their beliefs and interests dictate a secularist approach to public policy (indeed, much of the election rhetoric of Sharansky's party was directed against Shas). On the other, they tend to support hard-line foreign policies that conform to the preferences of the 'backlash coalition'. By the same token, the Arab parties, whose total Knesset representation increased from nine to ten seats, included a broad range of opinion, from universalists in the Communist Party through 'post-Zionists' in Balad to Islamists in the United Arab List. Moreover, the two largest parties both suffered significant losses: Labour fell from 34 to 26 seats and Likud from 32 to 19. In both cases, most of these losses were inflicted by smaller parties endorsing more articulate and strident 'internationalist' and 'backlash' messages respectively. The picture was further clouded by the fact that several Knesset members elected on lists identified with an 'internationalist' inclination had previously belonged to parties associated with a 'backlash' approach, suggesting that their own positions were more ambiguous than either their old or new affiliations would indicate.

Finally, Barak was unable to assemble a Knesset majority comprising just the Jewish parties of the natural 'internationalist' coalition. He rejected the option of making his majority dependent on the support of the Arab parties, since this would expose him to the charge that any future territorial concessions could not be approved without the endorsement of Arab voters in Israel. This left him no other choice but to include as junior partners 'backlash' members of the previous coalition – Shas (or Likud), the National

Religious Party and United Torah Judaism, which subsequently left the new coalition. While he was able to limit the influence of Shas, for example by forcing the resignation of its leader and depriving it of the Interior Ministry and the resources it controlled, this still meant that any 'internationalist' themes in his security and domestic policy had to be tempered by the need to accommodate the values of these partners.

This constraint took on added weight because of Barak's commitment to submit any peace agreements with Syria and the Palestinians to a referendum. While the mechanics and procedures of a referendum were not self-evident – there was neither a precedent nor a law to provide guidance – it was clear that demography would pose a challenge. Barak could proceed on the assumption that voters would be swayed in a more conciliatory direction if they were confronted with real, rather than hypothetical, choices, and that simple extrapolation from opinion polls was not necessarily a reliable guide to their behaviour in a referendum. Nevertheless, it was widely assumed that Shas' constituency would not eagerly support major territorial concessions without positive prodding from the party leadership. This was unlikely to be forthcoming without some accommodation of the leadership's 'backlash' agenda in domestic affairs. In addition, the 'Russian' voters, whatever their location on the 'internationalist'–'backlash' spectrum in domestic affairs, showed very little willingness to support territorial concessions, especially to Syria.[2]

The outcome of the 1999 elections thus provided an equivocal, but nonetheless suggestive, indication that Israel would begin to move, albeit cautiously, in the direction of what might be called 'limited internationalism'. That would imply the continuing liberalisation of the economy and entrenchment of civil rights. The Israeli Declaration of Independence committed the Constituent Assembly to adopt a Constitution no later than 1 October 1948. Even if that long-deferred commitment is still not met, there will probably be some effort to add to or amend the 11 Basic Laws ensuring the liberties and equality of citizens and to pass legislation to see their effective enforcement. Although a constitutional separation of religion and state is not imminent, there may well be some move to strengthen further the rule of law and to reform relations between religion and the state. This could involve restructuring the curricula and/or funding of religious educational institutions, reducing religiously inspired restrictions on individual economic activities, or changing the rules for military exemptions and deferrals for seminary students. Similar changes may also help to promote a greater sense of equality among Arab citizens. At the same time, there is little likelihood that they will culminate in Israel's renunciation of its Jewish mission, or in the full identification of Israeli Arabs with the Israeli polity.[3]

In matters of foreign policy, 'limited internationalism' will probably lead to more flexible Israeli positions on the outstanding issues in the peace process, especially territorial issues. That would facilitate, though not ensure, the achievement of contractual peace agreements with the Palestinians, Syria and Lebanon. In turn, this could pave the way for more cooperative political, economic and security relations in the region. There is little likelihood that this would produce even the very modest integration implied by the institutionalised exchanges of 'open regionalism', much less the deeper regional integration that is being pursued in Western Europe.[4] But it would at least encourage the kind of normal, mutually beneficial interaction based on routine contacts between governments and civil societies that prevails in most other parts of the world. In particular, it would permit more flexible regional alignments, allowing Israel to assume a role as a more normal partner in a less tense and dangerous system of Middle Eastern politics.

In security affairs, these changes would be reflected, after a transition period involving the upgrading of the IDF to compensate for territorial concessions, in a less nervous military posture and the adoption of a more balanced military doctrine. This doctrine would remain attuned to the need to deter or defeat a variety of potential threats – even Israeli 'internationalists' will not soon abandon the belief that military superiority is necessary to guarantee peace and security – but it would also rely more on defensive components and mechanisms of reassurance and confidence-building. This would be reflected, not in a revolutionary transformation of the character of the IDF or of army–society relations, but in incremental changes in the direction of a more professional military, serving a society less preoccupied with the primacy of security and devoting relatively fewer resources to it.

There is, of course, no certainty that even this modest version of 'limited internationalism' will prevail; the parliamentary balance of power is far too brittle to permit much confidence in any such projections. Even if it does prevail, 'limited internationalism' will not automatically bring in its train all the changes that it seems to imply. Much also depends on parallel developments elsewhere in the region. Even in the most favourable circumstances, it cannot ensure the fulfilment of some prophetic vision of tranquillity, prosperity and harmony, or produce a Middle Eastern version of the European Union. But it does hold the promise of more steady progress towards secure normality in Israel's second half-century of independence than could be dreamed of in the country's first 50 years.

Notes

Acknowledgements

The first draft of this Adelphi was written during the author's tenure as a Research Associate at the IISS in 1999. It benefited from the comments of the Directing Staff, and from discussions with other colleagues at the IISS and elsewhere. I would like to express my special thanks to three individuals. The first is the late Gerald Segal, who brought his special insights and personality to bear just before his fatal illness. His premature death is a sad loss, not only for his family, but also for his many friends and colleagues. The second is May Chartouni-Dubarry, whose invitation to participate in her project on Army–Society Relations in Israel at the Institut Français des Relations Internationales in Paris originally stimulated me to think about many of the issues discussed here, and whose critique of the manuscript helped to produce what I hope is an improved version. The third is Yezid Sayigh, my 'shepherd' at the IISS, who worked through several drafts and constantly prodded me to be just a little sharper and just a little clearer. Although we did not always see eye-to-eye, Yezid is the perfect example of a constructive critic, and I hope that I can return the favour. For any errors of fact or interpretation, I alone am responsible.

Chapter 1

[1] Parts of this and the following chapter draw on Mark A. Heller, 'Army/Society Relations in Israel: The Impact of External Factors', in May Chartouni-Dubarry (ed.), *The Israeli Changing Security Agenda: Army/Society Relations*, Les notes de L'ifri 10 (Paris: Institut Français des Relations Internationales, 1999), pp. 83–101.

[2] Amir Oren, 'From BG to Bibi: The Israel Defence Forces at 50', in *ibid.*, pp. 23–24.

[3] Uri Bar-Joseph, 'Variations on a Theme: The Conceptualization of Deterrence in Israeli Strategic Thinking', *Security Studies*, vol. 7, no. 3, Spring 1998, p. 147.

[4] The traditional security concept is extensively discussed in: Michael I. Handel, *Israel's Political Military Doctrine*, Occasional Papers in International Affairs 30 (Cambridge, MA: Harvard Center for International Affairs, July 1973); Ariel Levite, *Offense and Defense in Israeli Military Doctrine*, JCSS Study 12 (Jerusalem and Boulder, CO: The Jerusalem Post and Westview Press, 1989), chap. 2; Dan Horowitz, 'The Israeli Concept of National Security', in Avner Yaniv (ed.), *National Security and Democracy in Israel* (Boulder, CO and London: Lynne Rienner, 1993), pp. 11–31; Avi Kober, 'A Paradigm in Crisis? Israel's Doctrine of Military Decision', in Efraim Karsh (ed.), *Between War and Peace: Dilemmas of Israeli Security* (London: Frank Cass, 1996), pp. 188–211; and Yisrael Tal, *National Security: The Few against the Many* (Tel Aviv: Dvir, 1996) (Hebrew). See also Eliot A. Cohen, Michael J. Eisenstadt and Andrew J. Bacevich, 'Israel's Revolution in Security Affairs', *Survival*, vol. 40, no. 1, Spring 1998, pp. 48–50.

[5] David Ben-Gurion, quoted in Avner Yaniv, 'Non-Conventional Weapons and the Future of Arab–Israeli Deterrence', in Karsh (ed.), *Between War and Peace*, p. 144. Five decades later, Labour leader Ehud Barak was excoriated by his right-wing opponents for displaying the same kind of empathy, and suggesting that, if he were a young Palestinian, he too would have been a terrorist.

[6] The consensus on this issue, as on many others, has been challenged by a school of 'new historians'. Although these historians focus on Israeli–Palestinian relations before and during the Israeli War of Independence, some have addressed post-war developments, arguing that there were potential opportunities for peace in the late 1940s and early 1950s, especially with Syria. These opportunities, they contend, were not exploited because of Israeli reluctance. Such revisionist interpretations were not voiced in the critical, formative years of the state, and their impact in Israel even half a century later has been largely confined to academic circles; even here, they remain hotly contested. For an overview of the debate, see L. Carl Brown, 'State of Grace? Rethinking Israel's Founding Myths', *Foreign Affairs*, vol. 77, no. 4, July–August 1998, pp. 90–95.

[7] Yitzhak Rabin, 'Deterrence in an Israeli Security Context', in Aharon Klieman and Ariel Levite (eds), *Deterrence in the Middle East: Where Theory and Practice Converge* JCSS Study 2 (Tel Aviv: Jaffee Center for Strategic Studies, 1993), p. 9.

[8] Even after 1967, this doctrine became so ingrained and persistent that critics have labelled it 'archaic dogma'. Shimon Naveh, 'The Cult of the Offensive Preemption and Future Challenges for Israeli Operational Thought', in Karsh (ed.), *Between War and Peace*, p. 170.

[9] Sasson Sofer, *Zionism and the Foundations of Israeli Diplomacy* (Cambridge: Cambridge University Press, 1988), pp. 362–66. According to Sofer, this explains the generally contemptuous Israeli attitude towards diplomacy. Ironically, Diaspora Jews in distress were often found in countries, such as the Soviet Union or Iran, with which Israel had no diplomatic relations. This left Israel no choice but to rely on others to promote their well-being.

[10] During the period of waiting and diplomatic inactivity before the beginning of the June 1967 war,

Israelis sought relief from their anxiety in a popular song with the perversely reassuring title 'The Whole World Is against Us'.

[11] Alan Dowty, 'Israeli Foreign Policy and the Jewish Question', *Meria Journal*, vol. 3, no. 1, March 1998, www.biu.ac.il/SOC/besa/meria.html.

[12] Michael Brecher, *The Foreign Policy System of Israel: Setting, Images, Process* (London: Oxford University Press, 1972), pp. 549–51.

[13] Sofer, *Zionism and the Foundations of Israeli Diplomacy*, p. 380.

[14] Ze'ev Schiff, 'Fifty Years of Israeli Security: The Central Role of the Defense System', *Middle East Journal*, vol. 53, no. 3, Summer 1999, p. 438.

[15] Leon T. Hadar, 'Israel in the Post-Zionist Age: Being Normal and Loving It', *World Policy Journal*, vol. 16, no. 1, Spring 1999, p. 79; and Moshe Lissak, 'Civilian Components in the National Security Doctrine', in Yaniv, *National Security and Democracy*, pp. 64–69.

[16] Ben-Gurion, cited in Uri Ben-Eliezer, *L'Armée, la Société et la Nation-en-Armes*, Les Cahiers de L'Orient 54 (Paris: Société Française d'Edition, d'Impression et de Réalisation, 1999), p. 164.

[17] Brecher, *The Foreign Policy System of Israel*, p. 550.

[18] According to Bar-Joseph ('Variations on a Theme', p. 167), 'the May–June 1967 crisis represents the most severe case of specific deterrence failure in the history of the conflict'.

Chapter 2

[1] The classic analysis of changes in the relative defence burdens of Israel and the Arab states before 1967 is Nadav Safran, *From War to War: The Arab–Israeli Confrontation, 1948–1967* (New York: Pegasus, 1969), pp. 143–204.

[2] For a more detailed discussion of 'strategic parity', see Aharon Levran, 'The Military Balance between Syria and Israel', in Mark A. Heller (ed.), *The Middle East Military Balance 1985* (Jerusalem and Westview, CO: The Jerusalem Post and Westview Press, 1986), pp. 275–84.

[3] See Ian O. Lesser, Bruce R. Nardulli and Lory A. Arghavan, 'Sources of Conflict in the Greater Middle East', in Zalmay Khalilzad and Ian O. Lesser (eds), *Sources of Conflict in the 21st Century: Regional Futures and US Strategy* (Santa Monica, CA: RAND, 1998), pp. 177–91. On the specific problem of political succession, see Risa Brooks, *Political–Military Relations and the Stability of Arab Regimes*, Adelphi Paper 324 (Oxford: Oxford University Press for the IISS, 1998), pp. 55–72.

[4] The phrase Rabin used was 'Bli Bagatz u'bli Betselem' ('without the High Court of Justice or Betselem [an Israeli human-rights organisation]').

[5] See Gal Luft, 'The Palestinian Security Services: Between Police and Army', *Meria Journal*, vol. 3, no. 2, June 1999, www.biu.ac.il/SOC/besa.meria.html.

[6] See Ron Ben-Yishai, 'Military Intelligence Estimate: The Chance of War Next Year Is Greater than in the Past', *Yediot Aharonot*, 10 July 1998, pp. 6–9.

[7] Mark A. Heller, 'Coping with Missile Proliferation in the Middle East', *Orbis*, vol. 35, no. 1, Winter 1991, pp. 19–20.

[8] For a detailed study of proliferation in the Middle East, see Ian O. Lesser and Ashley J. Tellis, *Strategic Exposure: Proliferation*

around the Mediterranean (Santa Monica, CA: RAND, 1996).

9 Lieutenant-General Lester L. Lyles, Head of the United States Ballistic Missile Defense Organisation (BMDO), in an interview in *Israel Air Force Journal*, cited in Amos Harel, 'Israel Most Vulnerable to Ballistic Missiles', *Ha-aretz*, 25 August 1998.

10 Cohen, Eisenstadt and Bacevich, 'Israel's Revolution in Security Affairs', p. 50; and Amos Gilboa, 'Developments in Major Armies of the Middle East', in Mark A. Heller and Yiftah Shapir (eds), *The Middle East Military Balance, 1997* (New York: Columbia University Press, 1998).

Chapter 3

1 Michael Mandelbaum, 'Israel's Security Dilemma', *Orbis*, vol. 32, no. 3, Summer 1988, p. 358.

2 This term, which is often used to describe the modern State of Israel, connotes the re-establishment of the ancient Jewish link with the Land of Israel. The First Commonwealth lasted roughly from the consolidation of power by King David (1010–970 BC) until the conquest of Jerusalem in 586 BC. The Second was established following the return of Judaean exiles from Babylon in 539 BC. It ended with the destruction of the Second Temple by the Romans in 70 AD, and the dispersal of the Jews throughout the world.

3 It is not a coincidence that Ben-Gurion himself, in his retirement, was one of the first members of Israel's political élite to endorse the idea of the country's withdrawal from the territories captured in 1967 (with the exception of Jerusalem) in return for fully fledged peace treaties.

4 See Shmuel Sandler, *The State of Israel, the Land of Israel: The Statist and Ethnonational Dimensions of Foreign Policy* (Westport, CT and London: Greenwood Press, 1993), pp. 141–49.

5 During the late nineteenth and early twentieth centuries, proposed locations for a 'territorial' solution of the Jewish problem included Uganda, parts of Argentina and Birobizhan in the Soviet Union. There was even a whimsical idea to establish a state for Jews in Grand Island, New York.

6 Horowitz, 'The Israeli Concept of National Security', p. 30.

7 On Israel's reasons for launching the invasion, see Itamar Rabinovich, *The War for Lebanon, 1970–1985*, revised edition (Ithaca, NY and London: Cornell University Press, 1985), pp. 121–34.

8 See, for example, Emmanuel Wald, *The Curse of the Broken Vessels: The Twilight of Israeli Military and Political Power (1967–1982)* (Jerusalem and Tel Aviv: Shocken, 1987) (Hebrew).

9 This search for authenticity explains the constant Biblical references and encouragement of Bible study by Ben-Gurion, himself a thoroughly secular Jew.

10 Israeli Arabs, of course, were not immigrants, and the integration or non-integration patterns for them were quite different. But even for Israeli Arabs, it is noteworthy that most of the pre-1967 parties ostensibly formed to express their identity and interests were affiliates of the main Zionist parties, especially Mapai. The only 'genuine' Arab party was, in principle, a non-sectarian, ideological one – the Communist Party.

11 Magnus Norell, *Democracy and*

Dissent: The Case of an Israeli Peace Movement, Peace Now, PhD dissertation, Department of Political Science, University of Stockholm, 1998, p. 146.

[12] The 1999 elections even saw the first signs of regionalism, when the Negev Party ran unsuccessfully for the Knesset.

[13] Larry Derfner, 'The Mysterious Gini', *The Jerusalem Post*, 10 December 1999, p. B3.

[14] Central Bureau of Statistics, *Statistical Abstract of Israel 1999*, no. 50, Table 11.8, pp. 11–20; and Moti Bassok, 'The Wage Gap Isn't Shrinking', *Ha-aretz*, 21 December 1999. These figures refer only to salaried employees. If income from capital and self-employment were included, the gaps would be even wider.

[15] Yitzhak Mordechai, 'In Search of Security: Defending Israel into the Next Century', *Harvard International Review*, vol. 20, no. 2, Spring 1998, p. 58.

[16] In 1995, ultra-Orthodox women bore an average of seven children, as opposed to two among non-religious Jewish women. Michel Gurfinkiel, 'L'Etat Hébreu Survivra-t-il en 2020?', *Politique Internationale*, no. 83, Spring 1999, p. 187.

[17] According to Major-General Gideon Sheffer, the outgoing head of the Manpower Branch of the General Staff, only 45% of the annual cohort of 18-year-olds theoretically eligible for military service were actually recruited in 1998. Amos Harel, 'IDF Planning To Lower Maximum Age of Reserve Duty in Combat Units to 41', *Ha-aretz*, 7 September 1998. This shortfall was not, of course, solely attributable to the ultra-Orthodox. Much was also due to the fact that a larger pool of eligible candidates had made possible higher recruitment standards and a more liberal policy of deferrals and exemptions, especially for female soldiers. Nevertheless, between 1996 and 1998 the number of eligible men exempted for religious reasons nearly doubled, from 4.1% of the draft pool to 7.8%. Arieh O'Sullivan, 'New Approach to Motivation', *Jerusalem Post Magazine*, 12 November 1999, p. 12.

[18] Dov S. Zakheim, 'Economic Security after a Settlement: The Prospects for Israel', in Karsh (ed.), *Between War and Peace*, pp. 15–16.

[19] Shmuel Even, *Trends in Middle East Defence Expenditures in the 1980s*, JCSS Memorandum 54 (Tel Aviv: Jaffee Center for Strategic Studies, November 1999), pp. 9, 16–17 (Hebrew).

[20] Zakheim, 'Economic Security', p. 16.

[21] Gal Luft, 'Israel's Impending Revolution in Military Affairs', *Peacewatch*, no. 199, 4 March 1999, p. 1.

[22] Asher Arian, *Israeli Public Opinion on National Security 1998*, JCSS Memorandum 49 (Tel Aviv: Jaffee Center for Strategic Studies, July 1998), p. 38.

[23] Eetta Prince-Gibson, 'Self Service', *Jerusalem Post Magazine*, 12 November 1999, p. 10.

Chapter 4

[1] Ze'ev Schiff, 'New IDF Assessment Sees Regional Missiles as Main Threat to Israel', *Ha-aretz*, 5 May 1999. For analyses that predated the assessment of the Planning Branch and produced essentially the same conclusions, see Tal, *National Security*; and Mordechai, 'In Search of Security', pp. 54–59. Former Deputy Chief-of-

Staff Major-General Matan Vilna'i gave a similar assessment in a lecture at the Jaffee Center for Strategic Studies, Tel Aviv University, 28 June 1998.

[2] Tal, *National Security*, p. 224; interview with Major-General Yitzhak Ben-Israel, Director of Research and Development in the Israeli Ministry of Defence, *Defense News*, 17–23 August 1998, p. 22.

[3] Lieutenant-General Shaul Mofaz, 'The IDF Toward the Year 2000', *Strategic Assessment*, vol. 2, no. 2, October 1999, p. 10.

[4] Luft, 'Israel's Impending Revolution', pp. 1–2; Amnon Barzilai, 'The IDF's Third Arm', *Ha-aretz*, 23 April 2000, p. 5.

[5] 'Israel Begins Revolution To Modernize Its Military', *Defense News*, 22 March 1999, p. 8.

[6] Interview with Uzi Landau, 'A Critical Appraisal', *Ha-aretz*, 8 July 1999.

[7] Stuart Cohen, 'Israel's Three Strategic Challenges', *Middle East Quarterly*, vol. 6, no. 4, December 1999, pp. 42–43.

[8] The NSC was only the second item to be discussed in the Cabinet meeting that approved its formation. The first was the Cabinet's taking note of International Women's Day. *IIS News Flash*, Israel Foreign Ministry Information Department Website, www.mfa.gov.il, 7 March 1999.

[9] Gilboa, 'Developments in Major Armies of the Middle East'.

[10] 'Revamping of IDF To Include Thousands of Layoffs', *Ha-aretz*, 28 April 1999.

[11] The Treasury has demanded much more information about projected personnel reductions before it will release funds for severance pay. Moti Bassok, 'The War Over Defence Is On', *Ha-aretz*, 10 June 1999.

[12] 'Revamping of IDF'.

[13] Public-opinion polls show strong opposition to the idea of a volunteer army. Arian, *Israeli Public Opinion*, pp. 36–37.

Chapter 5

[1] See Etel Solingen, 'ASEAN, *Quo Vadis*? Domestic Coalitions and Regional Co-operation', *Contemporary Southeast Asia*, vol. 21, no. 1, April 1999, pp. 30–53.

[2] There are, of course, also Israeli Arabs – Muslims and Christians of different sects – who constitute almost 20% of the population and are part of overall Israeli culture, but not of Zionist culture.

[3] David Makovsky, 'The Dangers of Tribalism and the Missing Middle Ground', *Ha-aretz*, 30 April 1999.

[4] Martin Kramer, 'The Middle East, Old and New', *Daedalus*, vol. 126, no. 2, Spring 1997, p. 94. For a more elaborate description, see Maurice Kriegel, 'Israël à 50 Ans: Deux Idées de la Nation', *Politique Etrangère*, no. 2, Spring 1998, pp. 257–70.

[5] 'Poll: Most Israelis See PA as Genuine Peace Partner', *Jerusalem Post*, 17 March 1999.

[6] Hadar, 'Israel in the Post-Zionist Age', pp. 76–77; Kriegel, 'Israël à 50 Ans', p. 258; and Eliot A. Cohen, 'Israel after Heroism', *Foreign Affairs*, vol. 77, no. 6, November– December 1998, pp. 118–20.

[7] In a highly publicised incident in 1998, the anticipated appointment of a senior intelligence officer, himself religious, to the post of Head of the Intelligence Branch was blocked after he gave a newspaper interview in which he referred to non-observant Jews as 'Hebrew-speaking Gentiles'.

[8] Pnina Lahav, 'The Press and National Security', in Yaniv,

National Security and Democracy, p. 187.

[9] An e-mail poll in 1999 revealed that, despite majority support for the peace process, 73% of Israelis still believe that Israel will have to fight for its existence in another major war within the next decade. See *The Jerusalem Post*, 20 April 1999. Like the findings of most polls based on self-selected samples, this one should be treated with extreme caution. Nevertheless, its thrust almost certainly explains the finding of a more systematic study of attitudes towards freedom of speech and the media. This reveals that 43% of the Jewish public believe that more limitations should be placed on the media, and that 88% believe that state security should have priority over the public's 'right to know'. Relly Sa'ar, '43 Percent Favour Muzzling the Media', *Ha-aretz*, 26 May 1999.

[10] Attitudes towards the media may be a reasonably reliable indicator of overall attitudes on the legal–constitutional dimension of the culture conflict. There is a strong correlation between attitudes and socio-economic status: the religious and the poor are most in favour of restrictions on individual freedom of speech for the sake of the common good. *Ibid.*

[11] Whenever Orthodox forces in Israel have tried to push through legislation to withhold recognition of conversions performed by Conservative and Reform rabbis, the response among large blocs of American Jewry has been to lodge vigorous protests with the Israeli government. This pattern is almost certainly a predictor of more widespread alienation among US and other Diaspora Jews in the event of a 'backlash' triumph in Israel.

[12] Gurfinkiel, 'L'État Hébreu', pp. 197–98. Israeli responses to state-sponsored or state-tolerated terrorism in the 1950s and 1960s were much more aggressive in character.

[13] Official figures show the number of workers from the West Bank, Gaza and South Lebanon declining from 38,300 to 36,900 between 1994 and 1998, while the number of other foreign workers rose from 30,500 to 79,300 during the same period. *Statistical Abstract of Israel 1999*, Table 12.27, pp. 12–43. These figures do not take into account undocumented workers. About 100,000 Palestinians were working in Israel in 1999, while estimates of the number of foreign workers from other countries ranged from 200,000 to 300,000. Larry Derfner, 'Growing Apart', *Jerusalem Post*, 10 December 1999, p. B3.

[14] See, for example, Mehran Kamrava, 'What Stands between the Palestinians and Democracy?', *Middle East Quarterly*, vol. 6, no. 2, June 1999, pp. 3–7; and Glenn E. Robinson, 'The Growing Authoritarianism of the Arafat Regime', *Survival*, vol. 39, no. 2, Summer 1997, pp. 42–56.

Conclusion

[1] Another ethno-nationalist party, Moledet, remained outside the coalition.

[2] A survey by a Russian-language newspaper among immigrants from the former Soviet Union in early 2000 showed that 72% opposed any withdrawal on the Golan Heights, and 16% supported a partial withdrawal. Only 3% endorsed the complete withdrawal demanded by Syria as a condition

for peace. *Yediot Aharonot*, 14 April 2000, p. 4. The results of the survey may have been influenced by the suspension of Israeli–Syrian negotiations in early 2000, but the overall tendency is nevertheless clear.

[3] One telling indicator of this was that Prime Minister-elect Barak held gruelling negotiations with the ultra-religious parties in an attempt to lure them into the coalition while constraining their power and influence, but he held no formal negotiations with the Arab parties.

[4] On the concept of 'open regionalism', see Alvaro de Vasconcelos, 'Regionalisation of the International System', draft EuroMeSCo Working Group Paper on Integration and Subregional Co-operation in the Mediterranean, Rabat, 1998.

DATE DUE

GAYLORD			PRINTED IN U.S.A.